AI Powered Ecommerce Marketing

MASTER SEO, SCALE SALES CHANNELS AND DRIVE EXPONENTIAL GROWTH

By Greg Pilla

Contents

Introduction

Imagine a future where your ecommerce marketing ecosystem runs in perfect harmony and is powered by numerous AI intelligences. Multiple agents effortlessly handle ad campaigns, promotions, and real-time optimization for maximum profitability. Up-to-the-second analytics flow in, detailing every click, conversion, and campaign performance metric. AI-driven customer service resolves inquiries flawlessly, while automated SEO workflows tirelessly climb the rankings toward that coveted page one.

These AI assistants don't just execute tactics but continuously test new strategies, implement the winners, and report back learnings requiring minimal human involvement. This self-sustaining, AI-powered marketing nucleus keeps you informed through fully transparent data while exponentially growing your business.

While full AI marketing autonomy may still be over the horizon, we are remarkably close. Innovative companies are already thriving by combining the right AI-powered tools and cutting-edge strategies to unlock unprecedented capabilities.

This book will equip you with that same power. You'll gain a competitive edge by mastering the AI-driven tactics that ecommerce leaders use to achieve mindblowing growth today. More than that, you'll forge the path to developing your own self-sustaining, AI-powered marketing ecosystem realizing that visionary future that is on the verge of becoming reality.

This book is not an AI book. It's a book about ecommerce marketing in an era where AI is an integral part of the landscape. The narrative I've just painted is not mere fiction; it's a vivid depiction of the incredible growth opportunities that await when we harness a wealth of sophisticated tools. The good news is that while many companies, both large and small, may struggle to adapt, you have the opportunity to surge ahead. Others may proceed cautiously, but you will be the lightning that Thor commands, invigorating the might of his hammer. Wherever you are in your ecommerce journey, I'm now there alongside you. If you let me, we will no longer fly coach; instead, I'll bring you onto my rocket ship.

In the early days of our ecommerce journey, my two partners and I were three individuals with a website, a few products, and a grand vision. I had experience in direct sales, my partner Kym B had a background owning pilates studios, and my wife Degelis, our company's current CEO, brought expertise from the world of influencer agencies and her venture, TribeTats.com. TribeTats specialized in selling temporary tattoos online, gaining some traction and valuable insights into online marketing. Fueled by our collective knowledge and shared ambition, we embarked on a mission to revolutionize an industry by offering healthier alternatives to vapes, gummies, and wellness products. However, despite our best efforts, months and years passed without significant progress. We grappled with the notion that each new marketing strategy required full-time dedication to gauge effectiveness, leading us to constantly postpone crucial marketing channels like email marketing.

Fast-forward to the present. We've gained the confidence and expertise to implement any marketing strategy, whether through personal effort or outsourcing. We've mastered the art of staying ahead in the competitive landscape and sustaining explosive growth.

Looking back, we recognize the challenges we faced in the beginning, mainly the frustration of low traffic and the seemingly insurmountable goal of reaching certain revenue milestones. Through trial and error, we gradually learned the intricacies of ecommerce marketing, a journey that we could have significantly accelerated with the knowledge we possess today.

My heartfelt wish for you, the reader, is to achieve in a month what took me a year, and what took me five years to accomplish in just twelve months. This book is about speed, about condensing your growth by condensing your learning time. With this book as your guide, embark on a journey of rapid success and fulfillment, transforming your ecommerce aspirations into a thriving reality.

A particularly relevant story that comes to mind, unrelated to ecommerce but embodying the philosophy of "moving fast," is Derek Sivers's story about attending Berkeley College. Derek Sivers is a remarkable entrepreneur, life and business philosopher, and author of "Anything You Want" and "How to Live." Notably, he also established a highly successful ecommerce business called CD Baby during the early days of ecommerce.

Here is a paraphrased version of Derek Sivers' story about how "regular speed is for chumps" in his words. "When I got to Berklee College of Music, I was like a kid in a candy store. I was pretty obsessed with learning as much as possible, as fast as possible. I noticed something about the school: if you could prove that you already knew the material, you didn't have to sit through the class. You could just take the final exam and get the credit.

So, I thought, "Why sit through four months of classes if you can learn all the material on your own and take the final on day one?" And that's what I did. I started taking these challenging exams, one after the other.

People thought I was crazy. They'd say, "Why the rush, Derek? The regular pace is fine." But the regular pace seemed designed for the slowest students. I didn't want to base my pace on the slowest person; I wanted to go at my pace. So, while everyone else was doing their assignments, I was taking a final. By the end of my first year, I'd finished two years' worth of classes.

"Regular speed is for chumps," I'd say. It was like I was looking around, and everyone was walking, while I realized you could get on a bike and go a lot faster. That's how I lived my life at Berklee and how I've tried to live ever since. If you're doing what everyone else is doing, you're just a slowpoke.

In two and a half years, I graduated. It wasn't about getting out of school quickly; it was about learning directly. It was about setting your tempo and not wasting *a minute. Because, in the end, time is the most valuable thing we've got. Why spend more of it than you need to?"*

That is my wish for you, explosive ecommerce growth, ten times faster than your competitors, and ten times faster than you ever imagined you could grow.

The #1 Most Important Marketing Strategy and Why Everyone Is Lying To You

The reason most people pick up a book like this is because they have stalled. I know how you are feeling because I have been there many times myself. As a marketer, it's easy to get discouraged when things aren't going as planned. You may find yourself thinking thoughts like:

"My sales were flat this month despite my efforts."

"I want to try new strategies, but I can't seem to wrap my head around the budget for testing something new."

"The new strategies I'm interested in feel like a huge undertaking I don't have the bandwidth for right now."

"I'm frustrated because some of the tactics I'm trying and putting so much work into just aren't driving the sales results I was hoping for."

Then, with those frustrating feelings in mind, it's understandable that people often start looking to expand their knowledge and pick up some books on ecommerce marketing.

Many authors tend to frame topics in ways such as:

"The seven foolproof strategies that lead to success."

"The exact blueprint for ecommerce marketing success."

"The Step-by-Step Guide to Crushing Online Sales."

But over time, I realized these simplistic approaches were misleading. I want to tell you the truth, the kind that 99% of so-called "experts" won't say outright. This truth explains how the top 1% of successful ecommerce businesses are getting rich.

Let's address the elephant in the room first. There are no magic formulas or foolproof strategies for ecommerce success. This industry is a living, breathing entity, constantly evolving, leaving "guaranteed" tactics obsolete faster than the next algorithm update. What generates windfall profits today could be tanking businesses by next week. Even the most highly-regarded experts cannot offer bulletproof game plans. They lack intimate knowledge of your budget, skillset, email list size, or the latest marketing currents. Attempting to directly copy their approaches is a recipe for potential disaster.

Rather than claiming to be an infallible gospel, this book aims to be a trustworthy guide and decision-making toolkit. I will share the innovative strategies I'm actively testing and experimenting with. However, I will also transparently discuss their potential risks and pitfalls. I will acknowledge that specific tactics may not translate into home runs for your unique business. As I explain my thought processes behind implementing these strategies, you will get both sides, the promises and perils. More than prescriptive formulas, you will gain a compass for navigating ecommerce's ever-shifting landscapes. Together, we will pursue opportunities intelligently and realistically through critical thinking and data-driven analysis.

Now that you understand the dynamic nature of ecommerce marketing, the most critical strategy can be revealed...

The most crucial tactic is the SPEED at which you continuously TEST different marketing channels and strategies.

Imagine two similar businesses side-by-side. One tested five new approaches this past year, and the other tested 50. Which will likely find more success?

Testing within existing channels counts too. In email marketing, for example, you can test new templates, flows, segmentation strategies, and more. It all adds up. The key is rapidly testing both new channels and optimizations within current ones.

Through persistent testing, you'll determine what works for your unique business. Maybe Facebook ads are a winner for you or one of the many other tactics I'll cover. The point is to keep experimenting through a structured process to find profitable strategies.

The majority of your tests are expected to fail. But the few that succeed can take your business to the next level. You'll start ranking higher organically, paid channels will deliver floods of customers and further complement your organic traffic, and revenue will skyrocket. Testing gives you the data and insights to build a successful marketing framework tailored to your business.

The speed and consistency of testing and optimization are the most crucial factors for ecommerce marketing success. I'll provide tips and frameworks to help you test smarter and faster.

Earlier, I mentioned how we used to believe every marketing test required immense time and effort to assess potential profitability. This is somewhat accurate. You will need to put in hard work on each channel. However, some methods allow you to test rapidly and efficiently.

Continuous testing should become ingrained in your company's culture. It should not be viewed as a burden but as an ongoing process. Some may call it "iterative improvement." For more on that concept, I refer to Donna Meadows' classic book Thinking in Systems, which explores the idea that those with the tightest feedback loops gain an advantage.

The key is establishing processes to quickly test new strategies, gather data, learn, and optimize. With the right systems, testing can happen rapidly. You'll fail fast, learn fast, and find success faster. Testing should not feel like a slog but a constant flow of experimentation built into the core of your ecommerce business.

I'll share frameworks for testing efficiently at scale. The goal is to build momentum and run through many tests quickly to determine what resonates in your market. When testing is woven into your company's DNA, you'll gain an advantage over competitors without structured rapid testing processes.

Remember, while testing is crucial, the endgame isn't endless experimentation. We aim to build a scalable business that thrives on finding profitable channels quickly. By optimizing this process, you create a system that generates income, freeing you to pursue growth or even future ventures.

Here's the core concept:

1. Test relentlessly for profitability: Embrace lightning-fast testing of marketing channels. This iterative approach helps you discover what resonates with your audience and drives revenue.

2. Systematize and delegate: Once you identify winning channels, don't get stuck managing them forever. Build systems or delegate tasks to free up your time and energy. Consider hiring talent or utilizing AI tools to automate processes.

3. Repeat for exponential growth: As profitable channels generate income, reinvest in more testing and scaling. This virtuous cycle fuels explosive customer growth and amplifies your business's value.

4. Build for flexibility and exit: By creating a system-driven business, you gain the freedom to choose your future. Whether you envision growing further or exiting strategically, a well-oiled machine allows you to pursue your goals on your terms.

This formula, **Test - Systematize/Outsource - Repeat**, empowers you to:

- **Accelerate growth:** Uncover profitable channels fast and scale them efficiently.

- **Gain freedom:** Delegate tasks and build systems so your business runs without you.

- **Boost exit potential:** Create a valuable, well-structured business that is attractive to potential buyers.

Testing isn't just about finding profit; it's about building a scalable and sustainable business that empowers you to achieve your true vision.

Let's go into several approaches on how to do that.

First, what exactly is a test? A test serves two purposes:

1) Evaluate profitability

2) Assess statistical significance.

To test a marketing channel, try the new approach and analyze profitability. But what constitutes actual profitability?

Profit means accounting for ALL costs associated with the sale:

- Cost of goods sold

- Product packaging

- Fulfillment/shipping

- Labor

- Marketing expenses

- Agency fees (if applicable)

After subtracting every cost, if there's still positive profit left, only then is the channel genuinely profitable.

Many businesses only consider marginal costs directly tied to a sale. But to determine accurate profit levels, you must consider the entire cost structure, both direct and indirect. Leave nothing out; even peripheral costs play a role.

By understanding your complete expenses, you can accurately assess whether a marketing channel generates incremental profit. This clear-eyed view of profitability is critical for successful testing.

While seeing profits from a new marketing channel is excellent, we must ensure those results are more than just a lucky fluke. Enter **statistical significance**, your friend, in separating real success from random chance.

Think of it like judging a cooking competition. A dish might taste amazing, but was it a one-time triumph or consistently delicious? Statistical significance helps us confidently say, "Yep, this channel is truly making a difference!"

To figure out Statistic Significance or as I like to call "Finding Your Wow":

(1) Identify Your Star Metric: What's the key action you want people to take on your website or in your emails? Is it signing up for a newsletter, making a purchase, or downloading a guide? Choose the metric that directly reflects your marketing goal.

(2) Know Your Starting Point: Track your chosen metric for a week or two before launching the new channel. This becomes your baseline performance, something to compare against later. Imagine you usually get 100 website visits from organic search per day. That's your baseline!

(3) Unleash the Testing Tools: Dive into your analytics platforms to track changes after launching the new channel. Here are some powerful options:

- Google Analytics: See if your website traffic (or specific actions like purchases) increases after launching the new marketing campaign.

- Facebook Ads Manager: Compare conversion rates from Facebook ads to your website's average conversion rate.

- Social Media Analytics: Track engagement metrics like likes, shares, and comments on your social media posts to understand the new channel's impact.

(4) Interpret the Results: Most analytics platforms offer built-in "significance tests" or tools that analyze data with fancy terms like "p-value." Don't worry about memorizing those terms! Look for indicators like "statistically significant" or "likely due to the campaign." This tells you if the observed changes are driven by your new marketing efforts, not random fluctuations.

Remember: Profits and statistical significance are two sides of the same coin. Just because something's statistically significant doesn't guarantee it's profitable. Keep an eye on both aspects when evaluating your marketing channels!

Here's a pro tip to simplify your profitability goals per channel: **Find marketing channels that give you 2x ROAS**, but remember that "ROAS" should include all your costs, including agency fees, packaging, shipping, and everything else!

Think back to our discussion on actual profit. It wasn't just about revenue but about accounting for every expense involved in a sale. This applies perfectly to the 2x ROAS target, reflecting your actual bottom line.

So, how do we make ROAS truly represent our overall profitability? This shifts the thinking from "return on ad spend" to a broader "return on all expenses." Let's break it down:

ROAS = Revenue Generated / All Expenses

All Expenses include:

- Direct Costs: Cost of goods sold, packaging, fulfillment/shipping, labor.

- Marketing Expenses: Ad spend, agency fees, platform fees, design costs.

Now, why is this "all-inclusive" approach so important? Many businesses get caught focusing on just the direct ad spend or visible marketing costs. But those agency fees, fancy packaging for promotions, and even the extra shipping needed for higher sales volume? They all add up! Ignoring these hidden costs paints a misleading picture of a channel's profitability and can lead to wasted resources.

Here's a real-world example: Imagine a new social media campaign generating seemingly good returns. But digging deeper, you realize you haven't factored in agency fees, custom product packaging for the campaign, and increased shipping due to higher sales. Suddenly, that "profitable" campaign might not be so attractive anymore.

This underscores the importance of considering all costs for a 2x ROAS target. By consistently applying this principle, you prioritize channels that contribute to your bottom line. It's not just about generating revenue; it's about generating sustainable profit that fuels your business growth.

In rare cases, like discovering a platform with a remarkable 3x ROAS while minimizing fulfillment costs, achieving profitability becomes exceptionally clear. More commonly, partnering with an agency that streamlines processes, reduces overall expenses, and helps you achieve that 2x

ROAS target more efficiently can be a successful strategy. The path to marketing mastery is paved with data-driven decisions and a clear, holistic understanding of profit. Embrace the 2x ROAS principle, factor in all the costs, and watch your marketing efforts flourish.

Now that we have established a game plan for focusing on profitability and testing strategies in a small but statistically significant way, the next step in your high-level strategy is to incorporate leverage in three ways to further supercharge the speed of your marketing tests and implementation.

The three forms of leverage are: (1) Agencies, (2) Outsourcing, (3) AI.

AGENCIES. TO HIRE OR NOT TO HIRE. THAT IS THE QUESTION.

Approach 1: Leverage Agencies For Marketing Tests When Appropriate

Early in my entrepreneurial journey, an agency offering a peculiar deal crossed my path: no upfront fee, just a percentage of our sales for their SEO and marketing efforts. This "pay-for-performance" model resonated with me. Aligning incentives seemed like a win-win, fostering a true partnership.

However, months later, the honeymoon phase fizzled. Instead of an in-house team, the agency relied on several sub-agencies, each grappling with the notorious agency curse of limited bandwidth. While I might dedicate an entire day to SEO on specific occasions, they averaged a measly 10 hours per month on our account. This inherent imbalance felt unsustainable.

However, there were other issues besides the insufficient effort. Agency structures often involve varying employee skill levels. While some might be highly competent, others fall short. Unfortunately, a deep understanding of our business wasn't always guaranteed, leading to costly mistakes. For example, an agency writer published a blog post incorrectly labeling our gummies as unhealthy, which caused unnecessary damage to our brand.

This experience highlighted the double-edged sword of performance-based agency partnerships. While aligned incentives are attractive, sub-contracting challenges, limited attention, and inconsistent expertise can pose significant risks.

While my experience with agencies initially left a sour taste, outsourcing aspects of your marketing can be valuable. The key is to approach agencies strategically, aligning with the principles emphasized in this book.

Step 1: Channel Selection and Agency Evaluation

Start by choosing a marketing channel and decide whether to build it in-house or explore agencies. If considering agencies, interview several and observe their pitches closely. You might glean valuable insights applicable to your own efforts.

Step 2: Test Smart, Test Small

Agencies often propose hefty test budgets and timelines. Push back, suggesting smaller, statistically significant tests to ensure profitability first.

Step 3: Transparency and Alignment

Before partnering, discuss a clear path to profitability with the agency, including all costs, especially their retainer fees. Remember, profitability matters above all else.

Step 4: Learning and Managing

While some agencies disappoint, working with them can be a learning experience. Observe their processes and techniques to enhance your own understanding. Closely manage agency partnerships with regular progress reviews and in-depth analysis of their work, data, and cost/revenue figures.

Step 5: Value over "Brand Awareness"

Be wary of agencies overly focused on "brand awareness." This term often means burning your budget on vague top-of-funnel efforts. Prioritize agencies that care about driving measurable sales and tracking progress meticulously.

Step 6: The Right Fit for Each Stage

For each marketing test, decide whether to handle it yourself, involve an agency, or outsource later once the channel proves successful.

Remember, finding the right agency can be akin to unearthing diamonds in the rough. Applying these principles allows you to navigate the agency landscape, avoid costly pitfalls, and discover valuable partners that help you scale profitably.

Approach 2: Outsource

Outsourcing part or all of the work is another tactic to accelerate marketing tests and eventually scale campaigns. Beyond agencies, you can test freelancers and solopreneurs to manage efforts on your behalf.

There are many sites where you can find independent talent, especially after COVID expanded remote work. Platforms like Upwork, Freelancer.com, Fiverr, and others offer access to skilled individuals across marketing disciplines.

When outsourcing, I typically aim for affordable rates to maximize value. Traditionally, professionals in the Philippines have been a top option for English fluency and lower costs. India has vast talent pools, too, but you need to be diligent in vetting quality there.

I've had great success working with teams in Pakistan - the exchange rate allows very low hourly rates. My primary partner there is Sharif, who manages 200+ staff on diverse projects. Depending on the work, I pay only $5-8 per hour, and they handle large volumes with quality.

If you would like to be introduced to my preferred Pakistan team, email or send me a LinkedIn message with your project details, and I'll be happy to connect you.

Outsourcing shines as a strategic tool to amplify your marketing execution. It allows you to delegate tasks and accelerate testing and optimization. This efficiency boost ultimately translates to faster growth and a higher return on your marketing investment.

Approach 3: AI

This book advocates for rapid, intelligent testing across marketing channels. Excitingly, AI tools can further propel this approach. While the core focus remains on thoughtful testing and learning, AI can supercharge specific phases, enabling more, faster experiments.

AI's impact stretches across industries, especially ecommerce. Later chapters will offer step-by-step guides for conquering crucial channels like email and SEO, and everything I recommend can be done with AI. From generating email ideas and SEO techniques to implementation, system design, and plan execution, dedicated tools exist for each stage.

Furthermore, AI tools increase your reach and impact exponentially. AI can produce the work of entire teams in seconds versus weeks. It removes bottlenecks holding back experimentation velocity.

How do you integrate this into the book's core principle?

1. Test AI tools just like you test marketing channels.

2. Use them to manage entire channels or support your work within them. Ask AI models like ChatGPT, "What are the best AI tools for [channel]?"Then, test them!

3. Double down on effective tools, integrating them into your systems or outsourcing efforts.

Remember, it's not about using countless tools but finding and leveraging powerful ones to propel your marketing into hyperdrive.

Throughout the book, you'll find tool examples. Remember, new, better tools emerge constantly. Resources like https://supertools.therundown.ai/ curate the latest, and you can always ask Gemini, ChatGPT, or any AI model for recommendations.

Finally, AI can avoid getting stuck on concepts or implementation. If you don't understand something, ask a large language model (LLM) like ChatGPT or Gemini to gain clarity at an expert level in seconds.

Welcome to the golden age of AI, where you can achieve previously unimaginable feats. Make AI tools integral to everything you do and explode your business growth.

Ready to launch your ecommerce rocket ship? We've laid the groundwork, and this book is your comprehensive toolkit, packed with my hard-won knowledge and tactical secrets for dominating ecommerce marketing. You're in the driver's seat, so choose strategies that resonate with your business vision. Each tactic I share is an option, not an obligation, so don't be afraid to explore further innovative approaches.

Agencies, outsourcing, and AI tools are all potential allies. Experiment to see if they can turbocharge your execution, but always remember the core principle: speed is your fuel. Launch more tests, explore more channels, automate wherever possible, and prepare to witness your growth curve take off.

Success breeds success. When you find a goldmine, a strategy that turns $500 into $1000, dig deeper. Invest heavily in what works, but never get complacent. The digital landscape is a fickle beast, and relying solely on one or two channels can leave you vulnerable. Diversify! Test marketing channels relentlessly until you build a network of revenue streams, each feeding into the others.

Remember, growth requires focus. Systematize and outsource your winning channels. Free yourself to conquer new frontiers while your established engines hum smoothly. AI is your secret weapon. This book serves as your guide, but these powerful tools can accelerate your tests, giving you an edge over the competition.

Refrain from letting information overload hold you back. Take it one chapter at a time. Read, implement, and then return for more when you're ready. Remember, whether you're a first-time entrepreneur or a seasoned marketer, explosive growth is within your reach.

Embrace the challenge! By combining fun, rapid testing, and the power of AI, you can become the smartest, richest player in the game. Don't wait. Dive in and watch your ecommerce empire rise.

Chapter 1

The Thousands of Blogs Technique

Usually, books are ordered according to what makes the most sense to implement. Ditching the traditional playbook, we will jump right into a controversial AI marketing technique to highlight both the power of AI marketing and the decisions you will be forced to make to stay ahead of the competition and navigate the risks of AI.

There is a technique for generating thousands of articles with AI to skyrocket your SEO and potentially generate hundreds of thousands of unique visitors to your website each month. At a high level, you will be using an AI tool to create hundreds or thousands of articles specifically to improve your SEO.

First, find a scalable topic series based on your business or use AI software to help you identify topics. Imagine you're an ecommerce store selling outdoor gear. Using AI, you could generate thousands of articles covering topics like hiking trails in different regions, gear reviews and comparisons, camping tips and tricks, cooking recipes for the outdoors, and educational content about different outdoor activities.

The next step is to use title structures that can scale up to hundreds or thousands of total pages and create a list of keywords. The AI software I will suggest can also handle this step for you. Then, publish all articles at scale.

Utilize a site like byword.ai to produce SEO-optimized articles in a matter of hours with automated internal linking. The AI tool can also incorporate AI-generated featured images. Byword and similar tools can automatically publish to your website.

Once you've published your content, you can help search engines like Google discover it quickly, making it more likely for people to find your website when they search for relevant topics. Create a sitemap, which is essentially a map of your website for search engines that tells them where to find all your important pages and helps them understand how your site is structured. Luckily, platforms like Byword often generate sitemaps automatically. Then, submit your sitemap to Google Search Console, which acts as a communication tool between you and Google. By submitting your sitemap there, you're informing Google about your website and requesting that it visit and index all your new content. You can find instructions on how to do this on Google's website by searching for "submit sitemap to Google Search Console." Remember, this step is optional but can definitely help your content get seen by more people. If you're not comfortable with technical tasks, don't worry, it's not essential. However, it's worth considering if you want to give your website an extra boost.

The next step is to "edit later." Instead of meticulous pre-publication editing, prioritize publishing in bulk to quickly get your content out there. After 2-4 weeks, delve into Search Console data to identify URLs garnering clicks. Focus your editing efforts on these high-performing pages to maximize their impact and improve their conversion potential. Repeat this process every 2-4 weeks for new traffic-generating pages, ensuring your content remains fresh and engaging. There are sites doing this that are generating millions in monthly traffic.

Typically, you would edit articles and make them as high-quality as possible as you post them. This strategy involves letting AI write and publish articles on a large scale and then reviewing and enhancing the ones that are helping with your SEO and ranking. This method allows for a faster and more efficient process while still maintaining a high volume of content.

Now, let's explore the counterargument - in other words, why would you consider not doing this strategy? Strategies like this are so relevant because they could make you millions of dollars, zero dollars, or can actually hurt your business. The strategy beautifully highlights the power of AI. Pretty soon, most of your competitors will likely be trying these types of strategies.

However, it could just as easily backfire, so you must manage the risks of scaling AI strategies. When you start creating hundreds or thousands of landing pages, if it doesn't work out for any reason, it can be very annoying to undo and can cause some site structure problems if you need to undo it. For example, an agency we work with made a bunch of landing pages for direct-to-consumer ads, and then I had to unwind it with the help of our developer team when it didn't work. It was highly time-consuming and onerous.

The second risk of this strategy is that the search engine landscape is constantly evolving. Google and other platforms are shifting their stances on AI-generated content, posing a potential risk to its long-term viability.

On the byword website, in the FAQs, it says, "It's a common misconception that search engines like Google will penalize you for using AI content. While you may want to avoid AI detectors for other reasons, you generally don't need to do so for SEO." However, depending on when you read this book, that may or may not be accurate. Many AI tools are already popping up that help you avoid AI detection. Some examples are originality.ai and stealthgpt.ai, which help you generate AI content so that even AI detector software won't know you used AI. These tools wouldn't exist if specific platforms weren't starting to penalize you.

That said, while I was writing this book, Google seemed to flip-flop on its policy twice, first allowing more AI-generated content and then becoming much more conservative by penalizing AI content in a later algorithm update. So, this issue of AI content's acceptability seems to shift back and forth regularly.

Also, blog posts generally do a poor job of generating revenue compared to other SEO strategies, which we will discuss in detail in another chapter. However, this type of scale could potentially overcome that.

We are currently testing this type of strategy and actively considering all these issues. You need to do the same. Don't get overwhelmed; understand that these extraordinary AI strategies will emerge at a non-stop rate, and it's simple to test and consider the positives and negatives if you maintain an experimental approach to ecommerce marketing.

So, what is the answer? Do your research before conducting these AI-enhanced marketing tests to determine the current state of affairs and whether or not you will be penalized for using AI-generated content. In other words, run tests to figure it out! If you can pull off strategies like this at scale exceptionally quickly, you might blow away your competition, but you also might put your business at risk. This is extremely exciting. Don't shy away from it. Embrace it and continuously look into strategies like this one to decide if it makes sense to test while mitigating the risks.

While the ability to rapidly generate high volumes of content is undeniably powerful, the "Thousands of Blogs Technique" raises important concerns about Google's evolving stance on AI-generated copy. The search engine's latest core algorithm update specifically targets and penalizes websites containing purely machine-written content that lacks critical signals like author expertise, original insights, and clear evidence and sourcing.

Even if the AI output is optimized for SEO, inundating your site with automated articles could go against Google's quality thresholds, which prioritize experience and human authoritativeness. This risks negating any potential traffic gains by causing your rankings to plummet across the board. And once penalized, recovering from being labeled an AI content violator may prove immensely challenging.

To overcome this obstacle while still leveraging AI's content generation capabilities, you could implement complementary software like Originality.ai or StealthGPT. These tools can scan all your published content to detect any AI-written material, allowing you to filter it out before Google's algorithms potentially identify and penalize it. Combining an AI writing workflow with robust detection aims to increase the likelihood that you only publish human-authored or human-enhanced pieces aligning with Google's quality standards. This hybrid approach seeks to unlock AI's scalability while mitigating the risks of mass-producing pure machine output across your site.

The "Thousands of Blogs Technique" exemplifies AI's immense potential for scaling content creation and SEO efforts. However, it also serves as a cautionary tale about the importance of nuance and moderation when leveraging artificial intelligence. As Google's algorithms evolve to detect and penalize websites that are overdependent on pure machine-generated content, businesses must carefully weigh the risks against the rewards. Striking a balanced approach that combines AI's efficiency with human expertise, editorial oversight, and robust detection tools is likely the wisest path forward. Those able to harness AI's powers judiciously while adhering to search engine quality guidelines may gain a decisive competitive edge. While this cutting-edge strategy will demand continual monitoring and recalibration, those who embrace AI thoughtfully and responsibly can unlock game-changing opportunities to outpace their competition.

Resources from this chapter:

1. byword.ai

2. Originality AI: https://bit.ly/originality1

3. Stealth GPT AI: https://bit.ly/stealthgpt

Chapter 2

Email Marketing

Remember in the introduction where I confessed we procrastinated on email marketing for a year? It took us a few more years to master it, but the payoff was immense. Even with AI and shrinking attention spans, a well-maintained email list remains a gold mine in today's digital landscape.

Let me share the exact strategies we use. While we ultimately landed on Klaviyo for its user-friendliness and excellent deliverability, many fantastic email marketing tools exist. We initially used Drip but found that Klaviyo better fits our needs.

Capturing leads across your website is essential for growing your email list and nurturing potential customers. To maximize the effectiveness of your lead capture efforts, strategically place email capture forms in three key areas.

First, embedded forms should be placed throughout your website, allowing visitors to submit their email addresses easily. For example, you can include a form for subscribing to your newsletter. We recommend using Gravity Forms because it is more reliable than other plugins that may be prone to glitches.

Second, popups are an effective way to capture leads. These familiar windows appear after a set time or when visitors move their cursor toward the "close" button. Justuno is an excellent tool for creating popups, offering extensive customization options that lead to higher signup rates. We suggest using entry popups to offer discounts and exit popups to entice visitors with freebies, such as a "gummy with purchase!"

Finally, make it easy for customers to join your email list directly during checkout. By incorporating an opt-in option at the checkout stage, you can capture leads from customers who have already demonstrated an interest in your products or services.

By implementing these three lead capture strategies across your website, you can effectively grow your email list and nurture potential customers, ultimately increasing sales and customer loyalty.

Welcome Them with Open Arms (and Incentives):

New subscribers to your email list that were captured by popups should trigger a dedicated welcome series. For example, entry popups offering 15% off lead to a series focused on deals, while exit popups with freebie offers guide subscribers through relevant content.

By segmenting new leads based on their initial interaction, we tailor their welcome experience and maximize engagement. This personalized approach sets the stage for a long-lasting and mutually beneficial relationship.

Your welcome email series is crucial, so I'll explain exactly how to design an effective one.

The series typically starts with a welcome offer email. For those who don't convert from that initial offer, send a follow-up 24 hours later promoting your best-selling products.

One week later, send an email introducing your brand. The email should cover "Who We Are," "Meet the Founders," and your company's mission.

After another week, send an email showcasing your product variety and best-sellers.

Follow up with a gift-with-purchase promo email.

Finally, if someone still hasn't made a purchase by the end of the series, send a 24-hour flash sale email as a last attempt to convert them. This "flash sale" can offer existing promos or discounts rather than anything new.

The goal is to provide value, build relationships, and offer incentives to purchase throughout the series. Personalized and well-timed emails focusing on the customer experience perform best.

Once the initial warm-up is over, your email marketing journey continues! Klaviyo seamlessly integrates with platforms like WooCommerce and Shopify, unlocking a treasure trove of purchase history data. This goldmine reveals what people buy, their email click behaviors, and product interactions, all automatically captured and organized by Klaviyo.

Instead of relying on generic "spend over $125 and get a free product" offers, leverage Klaviyo's power to personalize these incentives and create a win-win scenario for you and your subscribers.

Harnessing Klaviyo's insights is a game-changer for your email marketing strategy. With this powerful tool, you no longer need to track or remember individual interactions with your customers manually. Klaviyo does the heavy lifting for you, showing you exactly who opened your email about hiking boots, for example, who clicked on a specific pair, and much more. This wealth of data allows you to understand your audience's interests and behaviors deeply.

Armed with Klaviyo's rich data, you can easily segment your audience into smaller groups with shared interests. Imagine creating a group of hiking enthusiasts who clicked on a particular pair of boots – this is the perfect audience for targeted offers. Klaviyo makes it simple to create these customized groups, enabling you to deliver highly relevant content and promotions to each segment.

Now comes the magic! With Klaviyo's detailed insights, you can craft personalized rewards that resonate with each group. For your hiking enthusiasts, consider offering a free pair of socks with their next boot purchase or a discount on a matching backpack. This laser-focused approach feels more unique and relevant to your customers, demonstrating that you understand their interests and value their business. By delivering such targeted rewards, you significantly boost your chances of generating repeat purchases and fostering long-term customer loyalty.

Remember, it's not just about the cost threshold of how much a customer spends; it's about building lasting relationships. By understanding and catering to individual preferences, you'll foster loyalty and ensure they keep coming back for more.

Throughout your email flows, you'll present various offers. We've found one of the most compelling options is to offer a free full-size product (rather than a small sample or travel size).

For example, "Spend over $125 and get a free product" performs better than simple discounts or other incentive types. Customers value getting an entire free item more than a percentage or dollar amount off. Full-size products allow them to properly try out a new item instead of getting a small sample that doesn't provide the complete experience. The free item also feels more personalized when it's based on their interests and past purchases.

Two other key email automations to set up are for abandoned carts and abandoned browse. If someone signed up for your email list but didn't add anything to their cart, you can still engage them. Send an email like "You have great taste! Here's 15% off those items you were checking out."

For shoppers who did add items to their cart but didn't complete checkout, trigger an abandoned cart email reminding them of what's in their cart and offer a discount or free shipping to incentivize purchase.

Automated emails like these bring back "lost" sales from shoppers who got distracted or changed their minds. A timely and relevant offer helps continue the relationship and capture their business. Test different timing and discount amounts to optimize recovery rates.

After a purchase, send customers a fun, memorable "thank you" email. Model it after entrepreneur Derek Sivers' legendary thank you email template, which went like this:

"Your CD has been gently lifted from our shelves by white-gloved cherubim and placed upon a satin pillow. A team of 50 inspected it and polished it to perfection before nestling it into a gold-lined box, handcrafted by monks in the hills of Kyoto. We lit a candle and hushed the crowd as our packing specialist tucked it safely into its cocoon. Afterward, we paraded down the streets of

Portland, where crowds waved banners wishing your package 'bon voyage!' Our private jet now whisks your order to you on wings of song. Thank you for shopping with us - your picture hangs on our wall as Customer of the Year. Though exhausted, we can't wait to see you again!"

Sivers says this quirky email brought him thousands of new customers. While it is tempting to focus only on big strategic moves when growing a business, tiny details that surprise and delight customers often generate the most word-of-mouth.

Feel free to tweak Derek's template and add your own flair. The goal is to stand out by surprising people with something fun and memorable. A unique thank-you email like this builds loyalty and gets recipients talking about your stellar customer experience.

After delivery, send a follow-up email to check that the order arrived safely and offer help with any issues. Include a form to contact your support team.

Once you confirm the customer is satisfied, send an email asking them to leave a review in exchange for loyalty points. We'll discuss review generation more later using a tool like Yotpo.

Send a "time to re-stock" email with related products or promotions one month after purchase.

In addition to these automated flows, send a promotional or new product launch email twice a month. Leverage your segmented list to only send product-specific deals to those most likely interested. This avoids wasting the time of uninterested subscribers and keeps your open and click-through rates high, boosting deliverability.

The key is sending timely, relevant offers tailored to each contact's interests. Automation makes this level of personalization possible across your entire list. The goal is to delight customers and incentivize repeat purchases through a mix of broadcasts and personalization.

When crafting emails, use entertaining templates that engage readers.

Start with a funny meme or joke to grab attention. Follow with the offer details and any relevant press features or educational content. Add a few customer reviews for social proof. End with another amusing meme and a link to your Instagram for more laughs.

The goal is entertaining readers, even if they don't convert on any particular offer. A bit of humor makes them less likely to unsubscribe because the emails are enjoyable rather than annoying. Leading with the offer lets interested contacts easily take action. Additional content caters to those wanting to learn more before deciding.

Don't overthink the humor too much. Look for memes or jokes related to your offer theme. Or browse funny content based on your interests until you find something that fits. You can also search for a comedian or celebrity who is naturally funny, such as Eddie Murphy, and search his meme catalog for one that aligns with your email goal.

The tone should be light and entertaining, like you're emailing friends. Make the offer clear, provide helpful info, and wrap it in humor. This formula balances promotion and engagement to build lasting relationships with subscribers.

We've covered designing effective email flows, but growing your list is crucial too.

While you can buy email lists, growing organically is often better. Purchased lists may hurt deliverability if those contacts don't genuinely want your emails. Bad email stats like low open and click rates can land you in spam folders.

Instead, focus on organic list growth through:

- SEO (covered in a future chapter)

- Social media (covered in a future chapter)

- Retargeting ads (covered in a future chapter)

- Referrals - Encourage existing customers to refer friends for discounts or rewards. This brings in qualified leads organically.

- Live events - Collect email signups in exchange for discounts on events, classes, or experiences related to your brand.

The goal is to collect contact info from qualified, engaged potential customers who want to hear from you. Avoid buying generic lists. Instead, use multiple strategies to grow your list with your ideal audience.

Auditing your email flows is a crucial task that should not be overlooked. Like a shiny new car, email flows require regular maintenance to ensure they perform at their best and deliver the desired results. When you launch an email flow, it may hum along smoothly, convert well, and meet all your expectations. However, neglecting to audit your flows can lead to costly consequences.

The cost of neglect can be significant. If you forget to check an email flow for months and it malfunctions, you could potentially lose thousands in missed revenue. Regular auditing prevents these costly missteps by identifying and addressing issues before they impact your bottom line.

Moreover, the email landscape constantly evolves, and what worked yesterday might not be optimal today. Regular audits allow you to identify outdated elements, optimize for changing trends, and keep your flows performing at their peak. This continuous improvement approach ensures that your email marketing efforts remain effective and relevant.

Audits also provide valuable data-driven insights into open rates, click-through rates, and conversions. Armed with this information, you can make informed decisions about A/B testing, segmenting your audience, and crafting even more effective campaigns. You can fine-tune your email flows by leveraging data to maximize their impact and ROI.

To make auditing a habit, schedule workflow reviews every few months. During these reviews, use the following checklist to ensure your flows are in top shape:

1. Check for conflicting automations, such as overlapping timings or triggers that might backfire. Ensure your flows complement each other rather than clash.

2. Fix any broken links or images that may create a frustrating experience for your subscribers, maintaining engagement and a positive user experience.

3. Verify that segmentation and tagging, the backbone of targeted campaigns, are working correctly to avoid sending the wrong message to the wrong people.

4. Monitor deliverability by monitoring spam reports and placement tests. Tweak content and design to improve open and click-through rates, ensuring your emails land in inboxes, not spam folders.

5. Dig deeper into the reasons people unsubscribe and address any recurring issues to prevent future losses.

6. Assess whether your automations still align with your audience's evolving interests and your business goals. Adapt and refine your flows to maintain relevance and effectiveness.

If you're new to Klaviyo and need help navigating the platform, several options are available to get you started on the right foot. One practical approach is to tap into the vast pool of experienced Klaviyo freelancers. These experts deeply understand the platform and can tailor their expertise to your specific needs. Whether you require assistance setting up your account, creating email flows, or optimizing your campaigns, freelancers can provide the guidance and support you need to succeed.

Another valuable resource for getting started with Klaviyo is the plethora of online courses available. These courses offer flexible learning at your own pace, allowing you to enhance your skills and knowledge on your own schedule. Many of these courses are designed by Klaviyo experts and cover a wide range of topics, from the basics of email marketing to advanced strategies for maximizing your ROI. By investing time in learning the ins and outs of Klaviyo, you'll be better equipped to create effective email campaigns that drive results for your business.

It's important to remember that auditing your email flows isn't a chore but rather an investment in the success of your business. By dedicating time to regular checkups, you ensure that your email flows remain healthy and happy and drive significant revenue. Just as you wouldn't neglect your car's maintenance, you shouldn't neglect the maintenance of your email marketing efforts. With the help of freelance experts and online courses, you can develop the skills and knowledge needed to keep your email flows running smoothly and effectively, ultimately leading to a more prosperous and profitable business.

➡ AI PRO TIP Finally, let's wrap up the plan to build a thriving email channel with an AI pro tip. There are so many great AI tools to help you with every aspect of email marketing. Tools such as Hoppy Copy are amazing tools that help you create emails and entire sequences and support you with everything you need for all your email campaigns. You can create anything you need in Hoppy Copy and paste it into Klaviyo, for example.

Another tool you should check out is AI-suggests, which instantly generates tons of ready-to-use content and new ideas for your business. This tool could help you come up with ideas for your funny emails.

Mastering email marketing is a journey that requires dedication, creativity, and a deep understanding of your audience. Throughout this book, we have explored the proven email marketing strategies that have contributed to our company's success. By implementing these critical steps, you can build meaningful relationships with your subscribers and drive significant revenue through tailored messaging and incentive programs.

To recap, start by building your list across multiple website touchpoints, such as popups, forms, and checkout opt-ins. Welcome new subscribers with a personalized intro series to make a solid first impression. Integrate your email marketing platform with your ecommerce system to access valuable purchase history data, allowing you to segment contacts based on behaviors and send targeted offers and recommendations. Craft entertaining email templates that blend promotions, education, social proof, and humor, avoid generic blasts, and embrace creativity. Set up automations for abandoned carts, browsed products, re-engagement, and more to deliver timely and relevant messages that win back lost sales. Grow your list organically through SEO, social media, referrals, retargeting ads, and live events, steering clear of purchasing generic lists. Regularly audit your workflows to identify improvements, adapt to trends, and optimize performance, treating it like a routine checkup. Finally, consider leveraging AI tools like Hoppy Copy for writing assistance and creative ideation, embracing technology to enhance your productivity and overall email marketing success.

Resources from this chapter:

1. Hoppy Copy: https://bit.ly/hoppycopy1

2. Justuno: https://www.justuno.com/

3. Klaviyo: https://www.klaviyo.com/

4. Gravity Forms: https://bit.ly/gravityforms3

Chapter 3

SEO

SEO offers endless optimization tactics, aligning perfectly with our core strategy of rapid testing. While the possibilities are vast, I'll share the specific SEO strategies that have worked best for our business so you can start implementing them right away.

There's nothing better than organic traffic - it's free and consists of people already searching for your offerings. Ranking on page one of Google for lucrative keywords can generate an avalanche of customers. The top three results for a high-value search term can drive millions in revenue for some companies.

Let's dive into the specific SEO strategies and tactics we leverage to continually improve our organic presence and rankings.

When creating a new page, first identify the primary keyword it should target. Then, use SEMrush to find related long-tail variations of that keyword and export them. To find additional opportunities, also export keywords from the top 3-5 ranking pages for that term.

Review all the exported keywords and pull out the most relevant ones for your page. The goal is to naturally incorporate these keywords throughout the page content. Aim to use the primary keyword at least three times, including in:

- Page title
- Meta title
- Meta description

- Image alt tags

- Page Content

Additionally, work secondary keywords into the page content where it flows well. Avoid awkwardly stuffing keywords - the language should read naturally.

This keyword research and optimization process applies to any new page, whether a product page, collection, blog post, or something else. It's also helpful in improving existing pages. Start by identifying untapped keywords, then update the content to target those terms strategically.

FAQs

One of the most effective SEO tactics is creating an FAQ section for every page you want to rank that targets relevant long-tail keywords. Use tools like SEMrush, industry knowledge, or AI generators to identify the questions your audience most wants answered about your offerings.

Craft thorough responses to each FAQ, seamlessly working in your primary keywords and related long-tail variations. For example, if you sell peanut butter and jelly sandwiches, naturally incorporate "p b and j," "peanut butter and jelly," and "how to make PB&J" etc. throughout the FAQ content.

You can leverage LLMs ChatGPT, Claude, or Gemini to instantly generate a list of FAQ ideas for the page and draft responses optimized for your target keywords. The AI handles the heavy lifting while you review and refine the final FAQ section.

An informative, keyword-optimized FAQ resource provides value to visitors while showcasing your expertise around high-value search terms. This multipurpose SEO and content marketing tactic will become an invaluable asset in driving organic traffic.

THE POWER OF BACKLINKS: YOUR WEBSITE'S POPULARITY TICKET

Imagine attending a vibrant networking event. Every handshake, every exchanged business card, signifies trust and value. These connections whisper, "This person is worth knowing." In the world of SEO, backlinks work similarly. They're digital endorsements, high-fives from other websites saying, "Hey, this site has valuable content."

But it's not just about quantity. The quality of your backlinks matters most. Imagine receiving a compliment from the most respected individual in the room – that's the power of a backlink from a high-authority website. Search engines take notice, perceiving it as a vote of confidence, boosting your website's credibility and ranking potential. And it's not just algorithms that benefit. Backlinks are clickable pathways that direct real people to your website and expand your audience reach. So, before we delve into the strategies, remember: backlinks are your digital ambassadors, advocating for your online presence and ensuring you're heard in the bustling marketplace of the internet.

Internal Link Building: Weaving a Web of Value

The first step is establishing a strong internal linking structure. Identify relevant pages within your website where users might find your primary keyword page interesting. Strategically use the keyword as anchor text in these links, seamlessly guiding users on a journey of discovery within your site. Consider phrases like "you might also like" or "explore this related topic" to encourage further engagement. For product pages, recommend complementary items on relevant pages.

External Backlinks: Earning Recognition Beyond Your Walls

For crucial pages, aim to secure external backlinks from authoritative websites. SEMrush can help you analyze top-ranking competitors and their backlink profiles. Use this information to set realistic and achievable long-term goals for your own backlink acquisition. Remember, consistent and sustained effort is critical – "regular speed is for chumps," as you rightly proclaim! I'll guide you in formulating a strategic plan to achieve your backlink targets.

One approach to acquiring backlinks is through press coverage. However, this method presents limitations in terms of control. You cannot dictate the number of backlinks you receive or the anchor text used by journalists and publications.

Therefore, as we'll explore in-depth later, we'll complement this approach by strategically leveraging overseas freelance guest posting services to diversify your backlink profile and exert greater control over its composition.

Platforms like Fiverr and Upwork host freelancers and offer such services. However, navigating their offerings requires diligence. Many promote guest posts on websites that are of questionable quality.

To ensure that we prioritize quality over quantity regarding backlinks, we have implemented a rigorous three-pronged vetting system. This process helps us filter through the noise and identify the most valuable opportunities for improving our website's search engine rankings.

The first aspect we consider is the website's authority score. We prioritize websites with an authority score that exceeds 30, ideally surpassing our own site's score. A high authority score indicates that Google trusts the website and that it has the potential to elevate our own website's ranking. By focusing on high-authority sites, we can maximize the impact of our backlinks and improve our search engine visibility.

Next, we look at the website's organic search traffic. We seek websites that attract at least 1,000 monthly organic visitors, with higher numbers being significantly better. If a website has zero traffic, it raises red flags and suggests that it may not be a valuable source of backlinks. Remember, websites without organic traction offer minimal SEO value, so it's essential to focus on sites with a proven track record of attracting visitors through search engines.

Finally, we consider the website's targeted audience. We favor websites with over 50% US traffic to ensure relevance and potential conversions. Targeting your core audience is essential for maximizing the impact of your backlinks.

If a website primarily attracts audiences from outside your target region, such as India, it may indicate bot-driven manipulation and potentially harm your SEO in the long run. By focusing on websites that align with your target audience, you can ensure that your backlinks are not only improving your search engine rankings but also driving relevant traffic to your site.

By implementing this three-pronged vetting system, we can confidently identify the most valuable backlink opportunities and avoid wasting time and resources on low-quality or irrelevant websites. This approach ensures that our SEO efforts are focused, effective, and aligned with our overall marketing goals.

Meeting these minimum thresholds is non-negotiable. We then compare these metrics to the offered price point and make a value judgment. Is the investment worth the potential gains? Remember, quality backlinks offer lasting SEO benefits, while low-quality links can even penalize your website.

While metrics are crucial, don't neglect qualitative factors. Look for websites thematically relevant to your own, featuring content that resonates with your target audience. Engaging, well-written guest posts on relevant websites provide far more value than simply chasing numbers. Combining a data-driven approach with qualitative analysis allows you to build a backlink profile that boosts your SEO and attracts the right visitors. While you now understand our proven backlink acquisition methods, the exciting world of AI offers additional tools to explore and integrate into your strategy.

Leveraging AI for backlink building can significantly streamline and optimize your SEO efforts. LinkHunter, while not necessarily AI-enhanced, is a powerful tool that automates outreach and sources relevant, high-quality websites within your niche. By fostering meaningful relationships through guest posting and partnership opportunities, LinkHunter helps you build a strong network of backlinks. The tool also offers additional features like 24/7 monitoring and automated internal link suggestions, providing comprehensive value to your backlink strategy.

For WordPress users, consider Link Whisper, a plugin that harnesses the power of AI to analyze your content and suggest optimal internal linking for improved SEO performance. With features like broken link repair, target keyword integration, and reporting capabilities, Link Whisper contributes to a well-rounded internal linking strategy, ensuring your website's structure is optimized for search engines and user experience.

Consider using the Monitor Backlinks AI Tool (SEO Optimer) to gain valuable insights into your backlink profile and competitive landscape. This AI-powered tool identifies the good, the bad, and the ugly in your backlink portfolio, offering actionable intelligence to guide your SEO optimization efforts. By analyzing your backlinks and comparing them to your competitors, Monitor Backlinks helps you make informed decisions about your link-building strategy.

Finally, similar to LinkHunter, you could consider using the Dibz AI Tool at dibz.me to streamline your link prospecting process by automating the finding and filtering of relevant website opportunities. By leveraging Dibz's AI capabilities, you can build a more robust backlink profile with increased efficiency, saving time and resources. The tool's intelligent algorithms identify websites that are most likely to provide high-quality backlinks, allowing you to focus on the opportunities that will yield the best results for your SEO campaign.

Outsourcing your backlink building efforts can be a strategic move to scale your SEO efforts effectively. As discussed in the introduction, outsourcing offers several benefits that can complement using AI tools in your backlink strategy.

Our company recently partnered with a small Romanian team specializing in backlink acquisition. This collaboration allowed us to leverage their expertise and resources to significantly scale our backlink-building efforts. The outsourced team follows the process outlined earlier in this book. Still, their larger workforce enables them to operate at a higher volume and in a more cost-effective way than we could manage internally.

Outsourcing backlink building offers several key advantages. Firstly, it provides scalability, allowing you to access a larger workforce and readily scale your backlink acquisition efforts without the constraints of internal resources. Secondly, outsourcing may be a more cost-efficient solution depending on your location and operational costs, particularly for high-volume campaigns. Additionally, partnering with experienced professionals can bring specialized knowledge and industry insights to your backlink strategy, enhancing its effectiveness. Finally, by freeing up your internal team, outsourcing allows them to focus on other core business functions, optimizing your overall productivity.

However, several important considerations should be kept in mind when outsourcing your backlink building. Quality control is crucial, and it's essential to establish clear quality standards and conduct a thorough vetting of potential outsourcing partners to ensure they meet your expectations. Maintaining open and effective communication with your outsourced team is vital for alignment and achieving successful results. Moreover, it's critical to ensure that your chosen partner adheres to ethical SEO principles to avoid jeopardizing your website's ranking and reputation.

Based on our experience, outsourcing backlink building has proven to be a valuable approach. However, the best strategy ultimately depends on your specific needs and resources. Carefully weighing the advantages and considerations outlined above will help you determine if outsourcing aligns with your goals and values. Outsourcing can be a powerful tool in your SEO arsenal by making an informed decision and selecting a reliable partner, enabling you to scale your backlink building efforts and achieve long-term success in search engine rankings.

Avoid Focusing Too Much On Blogs

Regarding SEO, many agencies overly prioritize blog content over-optimizing product and collection pages. While blogs can provide informational value, ecommerce sites should focus first on ranking their shoppable pages to drive sales.

Blogs often target non-transactional keywords that bring site traffic without purchases. This increases server load without revenue. Meanwhile, product and collection pages have a clear purchase intent. Ranking them for commercial keywords directly drives sales.

Some agencies push endless blogs to keep clients locked into content production retainers. But with AI, you can create blogs exponentially faster.

The priority should be allocating time and resources to optimize and promote shoppable pages.

Of course, relevant blog posts still have benefits like increasing time on site, building trust, and enabling internal linking. I recommend one optimized blog for each core product, then shifting focus to ranking product pages themselves.

The critical takeaway is keeping your goals in sight. Traffic and backlinks are a means to an end. For ecommerce sites, that end is sales. Keep your SEO efforts centered on capturing purchase-ready searchers, not just informational surfers. Product and collection pages are the vehicles to get you there. With all that being said, the first chapter of this book contradicts this recommendation. It is possible that a massive amount of blogs can overcome the shortcomings mentioned here. However, you now have all the knowledge to make fast decisions when executing your content strategy.

REVIEWS FOR SEO

Customer reviews are a powerful tool that can significantly boost your SEO efforts and drive conversions. These reviews offer unique benefits that can elevate your product pages and attract potential customers. By naturally incorporating relevant keywords that you might have overlooked, reviews provide an SEO boost through organic keyword usage. As customers share their experiences and highlight specific product features, they utilize a diverse vocabulary, enriching your content with terms that potential buyers might use when searching for products like yours. This organic keyword inclusion enhances your product pages' visibility in search results, making it easier for interested customers to find and engage with your offerings.

However, the true power of reviews goes beyond SEO. They hold the key to transforming your product descriptions into conversion powerhouses. Once you have accumulated a substantial number of reviews, take the time to analyze them carefully. Pay attention to recurring themes, positive mentions of product features, and the benefits that customers frequently highlight. These insights provide invaluable information about what your customers value most and how they perceive your products.

Armed with this knowledge, you can harness your customers' voices to rewrite your product descriptions for maximum impact. By incorporating your customers' language and enthusiasm to express value, you create descriptions that resonate deeply with potential buyers. Weave in the benefits that customers find most compelling and highlight the features that they appreciate the most. This approach fosters trust, clarifies the value proposition of your products, and ultimately drives conversions by speaking directly to the needs and desires of your target audience.

When leveraging customer reviews to enhance your product descriptions, maintaining authenticity is essential. Rather than simply copy-pasting excerpts from reviews, craft a seamless narrative that incorporates customer insights while preserving a consistent brand voice. This approach ensures your descriptions feel genuine and relatable, further building trust with potential customers.

Remember, rewriting product descriptions based on customer reviews doesn't have to be overwhelming. You can always leverage the power of language models (LLMs) to assist you in this process. These AI-driven tools can help you analyze reviews, identify key themes, and generate compelling descriptions that seamlessly integrate customer insights.

By harnessing the SEO and conversion benefits of customer reviews, you can create product pages that rank well in search results and effectively persuade potential customers to make a purchase. Embrace your customers' voices, and let their authentic experiences and opinions guide your product descriptions to new heights of success.

➡ AI PRO TIP Rather than manually implementing SEO tactics, which can be time-consuming and resource-intensive, consider harnessing the power of AI tools to automate processes and generate optimized content at scale. Platforms like Mango SEO offer comprehensive SEO solutions explicitly designed for rapid growth, enabling you to achieve your SEO goals more efficiently and effectively.

One of Mango SEO's key advantages is its seamless integration with WordPress, allowing you to create unlimited AI-generated content that is optimized for your target keywords. By leveraging SEMrush's API for real-time keyword data, Mango SEO ensures that your content always aligns with the latest search trends and user queries. This powerful integration enables you to establish automated, optimized content workflows around every relevant keyword and keyphrase, saving you valuable time and effort while maximizing your SEO impact.

In addition to its content generation capabilities, Mango SEO offers a wide range of features designed to streamline your SEO efforts. The platform provides comprehensive SEO audits identifying potential issues and optimization opportunities, helping you prioritize your efforts for maximum impact. It also generates AI-powered meta titles and descriptions, optimizes images for search engines, recommends internal linking strategies, and conducts competitive analysis to keep you ahead of the curve. With ongoing rank tracking, you can monitor your progress and adjust your strategy as needed to ensure continuous improvement.

By leveraging AI tools like Mango SEO, you can achieve fully automated, data-driven SEO without the typical time investment required by manual efforts. These advanced platforms handle repetitive tasks with precision and efficiency, allowing you to focus on high-level strategy and other critical aspects of your business. The technology takes care of the tedious, time-consuming work, freeing you up to concentrate on the bigger picture and driving your SEO success to new heights.

In closing, SEO is a must for inbound marketing and business growth. While it takes commitment, the return on investment is tremendous. Compared to paid ads, every organic visitor costs nothing to acquire, and their value compounds over time.

Get excited about dominating the rankings through extensive keyword research, technical optimizations, stellar content, and link-building. Then, unlock lightning-fast results by deploying amazing AI tools that automate SEO processes.

With relentless focus and execution, you can realistically conquer page one for your most important keywords within months rather than years. The flood of free, qualified website traffic will rapidly accelerate your business. SEO success takes work but brings unmatched rewards. I'm eager to help you maximize your organic presence - let's start building your SEO empire today!

<u>Resources from this chapter:</u>

1. Dibz.me: https://dibz.me/

2. Link Whisper: https://bit.ly/linkwhisper1

3. Link Hunter: https://linkhunter.io/

4. Mango SEO: https://bit.ly/MangoSEO

5. Monitor Backlinks (SEO Optimer): https://monitorbacklinks.com/

6. SEM rush: https://www.semrush.com/

Chapter 4

PR

Public relations wasn't just a marketing tactic for us; it was a game-changer. For example, our early feature in Allure magazine generated a staggering $15,000 per month in sales for years after its publication.

The reach of major publications provides immense exposure. Their high-authority articles often rank at the top for valuable keywords, sending you loads of qualified visitors. For example, a Forbes piece titled "Best Wellness Gummies" could dominate that search, funneling interested shoppers your way if included.

Beyond traffic and links, press offers credibility that builds trust. Being featured editorially feels like an endorsement, much more so than advertising. It establishes you as an authority in readers' eyes.

Doing PR in-house can be effective before considering agency partnerships. Tools like MuckRack provide journalist databases to identify and contact relevant media. (I'll mention some additional platforms to consider at the end of this chapter)

Search for writers who recently covered topics or competitors in your space. Check for their contact information so you can pitch ideas directly. Avoid generic pitches - craft compelling narratives tailored to their audience and beat.

Pitch reporters story ideas framed around your brand as the central character - such as an entrepreneurial journey, unique product development, or new funding announcement. Support pitches with data and angles catered to each outlet.

Persistently follow up with those who express interest or request more information. Building relationships takes time but increases the likelihood of coverage.

While agencies tout media connections, many simply blast impersonal emails lacking substance. By taking a targeted, personal approach yourself, you can likely land major coverage and save on agency fees.

Once you gain initial press traction, consider hiring a firm at that point to support PR at scale. But don't underestimate what you can achieve through your own hustle and intelligent outreach. With the right strategy, securing articles in top-tier publications is very possible.

While the methods outlined previously provide a solid foundation, consider venturing beyond them to unlock additional PR opportunities. There are a few unconventional yet effective strategies.

Leveraging social media platforms like Instagram can be an effective way to connect with relevant journalists and secure media coverage. Reporters increasingly maintain an active social media presence, and Instagram provides an opportunity to reach out directly. Craft personalized direct messages highlighting your product's value proposition and potential relevance to their readership. Remember to strategically offer free samples or products, ensuring alignment with their audience's needs.

However, securing PR coverage often requires persistent and personalized efforts, similar to sales outreach. Don't be discouraged by initial silence; multiple emails and contact points might be necessary. Persistence, coupled with respectful follow-up, can increase your chances of success.

Participating in speaking engagements can also be a valuable strategy for amplifying your voice and gaining media attention. These events position you as an industry expert and thought leader, often offering opportunities to connect with journalists and media professionals, fostering potential coverage and backlink acquisition. Seek speaking slots at conferences, webinars, or relevant industry gatherings.

Sponsoring initiatives like charity events can also yield valuable backlinks. Many charities offer website mentions or dedicated pages for their sponsors. Additionally, explore opportunities to request website backlinks when sponsoring relevant events or projects.

While DIY PR and agency partnerships are valuable approaches, another method worth exploring is strategic placement targeting top-ranking articles. This approach recognizes the potent link-building power of PR but also aims for articles that drive direct revenue. The focus is on securing placements in articles that are already ranking on Google's first or second page for keywords crucial to your business.

Imagine searching for "best XYC product" and finding multiple articles on top pages. These highly visible pieces represent PR goldmines. By identifying publications with such articles and pitching them a unique angle featuring a similar product, you can leverage their established ranking potential while maintaining relevance to their audience. Author bios typically reveal the writer or publishing company behind these articles, and you can also utilize AI tools to unearth contact information. Armed with this knowledge, reach out and propose inclusion in future pieces, offering samples or exploring paid arrangements depending on their policies.

This approach offers several advantages. Firstly, securing placement in articles that are already ranking for relevant keywords drives targeted traffic directly interested in your product category. Secondly, you gain a high-quality backlink from a website with solid SEO performance. Additionally, relevantly placed product mentions within established content tend to attract higher click-through rates compared to generic press releases.

By strategically leveraging top-ranking articles, you can unlock a powerful PR approach that generates qualified leads, builds valuable backlinks, and fuels your SEO success. Remember, this method should complement your existing PR efforts, not replace them.

Hiring PR Agencies

If you have a budget, it's great to test hiring PR agencies at times when you can't work on PR yourself. PR agencies can secure major coverage initially by tapping their media relationships. However, results often dwindle after the first 6-12 months when they exhaust their rolodex.

We've found most agencies front-load their best journalist connections early on. After the initial burst, performance decreases without insider access to maintain exclusives.

A potential strategy is cycling through agencies on 6-12 month contracts. For that first stretch, their connections will land major placements. Renegotiate or switch for fresh relationships to restart momentum.

Look for agencies founded by ex-journalists boasting strong personal ties or boutiques with proven, narrow focuses. Avoid vague promises of general media access. Vet case studies and quantify results.

While not a long-term solution, short-term agency partnerships maximize the value of connections before they're depleted. Sustained PR requires constantly expanding your media network.

Streamline PR Efforts with AI

▶ **AI PRO TIP** Rather than relying solely on manual outreach or hiring agencies, consider leveraging AI tools to automate and enhance your PR processes. Platforms like JustReachOut, Intelligent Relations, and Cision provide robust capabilities to non-technical users, making it easier to streamline and scale your PR efforts.

These tools offer a comprehensive suite of features, including a vast media database of hundreds of thousands of journalists, outlets, and influencers. Additionally, they harness AI-powered pitch writing tailored to each target, enabling you to craft compelling narratives that resonate with your desired audience. Automated personalized outreach at scale is another key advantage, allowing you to efficiently reach a wide range of media professionals without sacrificing personalization.

Furthermore, these platforms provide relationship management tools to track engagement and monitor the impact of your outreach efforts. Comprehensive monitoring and analytics of coverage ensure that you can measure the success of your campaigns and make data-driven decisions.

One of the most significant benefits of AI PR software is its cost-effectiveness. With pricing starting at around $500 per month, these tools offer a fraction of the cost of traditional agency services. They streamline the process by identifying ideal press targets, drafting compelling pitches, and handling follow-ups automatically, reducing the need for manual intervention and freeing up your team to focus on high-level PR strategy.

AI eliminates the grunt work associated with PR outreach while optimizing the effectiveness of your campaigns. The technology handles repetitive tasks, allowing you to concentrate on developing and executing sophisticated PR strategies that were once the exclusive domain of agencies.

As the PR landscape evolves, consider testing AI PR software to accelerate your outreach efforts and increase the likelihood of landing valuable placements. These powerful platforms represent the future of efficient, automated earned media, empowering small teams to achieve results previously reserved for those with substantial agency budgets.

Public relations is a powerful tool that extends far beyond just brand awareness and credibility. Successful PR campaigns can fuel your SEO efforts by driving qualified traffic from high-authority publications ranking for valuable keywords. Additionally, securing editorial mentions and backlinks from these authoritative sources boosts your website's search engine visibility and domain authority. By strategically leveraging PR to land placements in top-ranking articles, you not only gain exposure to a targeted audience but also reap the long-term benefits of improved organic search performance. As you execute your PR initiatives, remember that each earned media opportunity has the potential to amplify your online presence and drive sustained growth through enhanced search engine optimization.

Resources from this chapter:

1. Muck Rack: https://muckrack.com/

2. Just Reach Out: https://justreachout.io/

3. Intelligent Relations: https://www.intelligentrelations.com/

4. Cision: https://www.cision.com/

Chapter 5

Affiliate

If you hire an affiliate agency, they will mostly just sign you up on coupon sites that don't actually increase sales. These sites provide coupons to people who already shop on your site.

At the end of the day, the best way to grow your affiliate channel is through PR since most publications now include affiliate links in their content. The media industry is struggling, so publications are looking for new revenue streams.

There are some review sites specific to your vertical that can be good affiliate partners. For example, if you sell mattresses, there are probably websites like "MattressesReviews.com" which will review your product and include an affiliate link.

But overall, affiliate growth is really a byproduct of your broader efforts in press, influencer marketing, and other areas where partners naturally use affiliate links. In our experience, affiliates shouldn't be siloed but rather integrated into your overall strategy.

After trying out a few software options, we recommend ShareASale due to its relatively low setup costs and extensive publisher network.

In summary, get yourself set up with an affiliate network, but focus on PR and invite potential partners to join your program when they are going to promote your product anyway. Growing your affiliate channel means growing your overall presence and partnerships. In our experience, we found that "growing our affiliate channel" really means "growing our press."

I'm not highly bullish on affiliate marketing since much of its success is driven by broader press and PR efforts, which we have covered in the previous chapter. However, it can still be an extraordinarily successful channel for your specific business. A channel that was just mediocre for my company could be explosive for yours. It's essential to analyze each marketing channel's pros and cons objectively.

Affiliate marketing can be powerful for cost-effectively driving sales if approached strategically. While relying solely on coupon sites and passive efforts yielded pitfalls, in my experience, a proactive and diversified affiliate strategy can produce much better results. Let's get into a plan for building a successful affiliate program.

1. DIVERSIFY YOUR AFFILIATE PARTNER TYPES

When building your affiliate program, it is crucial to diversify your affiliate partner types beyond just coupon and deal sites. You can significantly expand your reach and credibility by recruiting a wide range of partners.

First, actively seek out reputable bloggers and content creators within your niche. These influencers can provide in-depth reviews, tutorials, and ongoing coverage of your products to their loyal audiences. Platforms like Tomoson or agencies like NeoReach can help you identify and connect with relevant content creators. An AI-powered platform like Klear can further streamline influencer discovery and outreach.

Influencers and thought leaders with large mainstream followings should also be tapped to showcase your brand to new demographics. An influencer marketing platform like Traackr enables you to search for influencers based on demographics, interests, reach, and more. The AI tools can help match you with ideal partners. (In the next chapter, we will dive much deeper into influencer marketing, which compliments your affiliate marketing.)

Remember to collaborate with authoritative review sites and publications that align with your industry. Providing them with products to test and detailed information will encourage comprehensive reviews. You can use tools like Buzzsumo to find the top content creators around your product's keywords.

And finally, industry experts and advisors can provide key credibility as affiliates even if they aren't stereotypical influencers.

By diversifying instead of limiting your program to deal sites, you can unlock your affiliate channel's full potential to drive awareness, trust, and sales through strategic partnerships.

2. UTILIZE ADVANCED AFFILIATE MARKETING TOOLS

➡ AI PRO TIP You should explore AI-powered platforms like Affistash and Publisher Discovery to take your affiliate marketing efforts to new heights. These innovative solutions leverage cutting-edge AI technology to streamline every aspect of affiliate outreach and management.

Affistash and Publisher Discovery can automatically discover relevant affiliates across the web, analyze their performance and audience fit, and provide you with verified contact details to initiate partnerships. By harnessing the power of AI, you can bypass the traditional manual processes involved in affiliate marketing and take a more proactive, data-driven approach to building and optimizing your affiliate program.

Whether you're just starting with affiliate marketing or looking to take your existing program to the next level, Affistash and Publisher Discovery offer comprehensive solutions tailored to help you maximize the growth and ROI of your affiliate channel. Leveraging AI in this way can give you a significant competitive advantage and enable you to stay ahead of the curve in the ever-evolving world of affiliate marketing.

Resources from this chapter:

1. Share A Sale: https://www.shareasale.com/

2. Tomoson: https://www.tomoson.com/

3. NeoReach: https://neoreach.com/

4. Klear (Meltwater): https://www.meltwater.com/en

5. Traackr: https://www.traackr.com/

6. BuzzSumo: https://buzzsumo.com/

7. Affistash: https://bit.ly/affistash

8. Publisher Discovery: https://www.publisherdiscovery.com/

Chapter 6

Reviews and Yotpo

Did you know that 93% of consumers read online reviews before making a purchase, according to a 2023 PowerReviews study? In today's competitive landscape, positive reviews are essential for building trust and attracting customers.

Building trust and positive word-of-mouth is crucial for any business, especially in competitive markets. Collecting customer reviews from day one, even before becoming a giant, helps establish credibility and attract new customers. Think of it as building a foundation of trust.

Consider Yotpo, a leading review management platform. Yotpo offers robust features like review moderation, automated email requests, and social media integration to help you manage your online reputation effectively. Still, Yotpo is very expensive, so unless you are funded, it might be better to start collecting reviews and transfer them over to Yotpo once you're bigger. Start by simply encouraging reviews through email, social media, or on your website. As you grow, migrating to a robust platform like Yotpo becomes more feasible. Explore free or affordable alternatives like Google Customer Reviews, Trustpilot, or Shopify's built-in review system.

Our Yotpo package combines reviews, loyalty programs, and referral programs (like "refer a friend and earn $20"). Loyalty programs incentivize repeat business. One example is that my wife can get makeup and skincare products anywhere, but she loves to shop at Sephora because they always have free stuff for their loyalty program members at checkout. Our loyalty program offers 10% cash back and points redeemable for discounts.

We like that Yotpo integrates seamlessly with Klaviyo, our email marketing platform. This allows us to reach customers with personalized messages about their loyalty rewards.

Imagine a customer who raves about your product's unique feature in a Yotpo review and mentions their desire to explore another product from the same line. What if you could leverage this valuable feedback and their loyalty status to create a personalized experience that delights them further? The magic happens through the seamless integration of Yotpo and Klaviyo. When a customer leaves a positive review, Yotpo automatically identifies key details like product mentions and their loyalty tier. This information can seamlessly flow into Klaviyo, triggering a personalized email campaign that you set up.

The email doesn't just thank them for the review—it speaks their language. It highlights their positive feedback and recommends the product they mentioned, sweetened with a loyalty-specific perk. Perhaps it offers bonus points for trying the recommended product or an exclusive discount as a valued member. Additionally, the email might suggest other products from the same line based on their review and preferences, creating a truly curated experience.

This personalized approach is a win-win. Customers feel valued and understood, increasing their engagement and loyalty. Incentivizing reviews with points and tailoring recommendations drives sales and fosters a community of brand advocates. It's a testament to the power of integrating review management with email marketing, unlocking a personalized journey that rewards your customers and your business.

Whether you're a DIY whiz or crave expert guidance, you can unlock personalized loyalty rewards with Yotpo reviews. Explore Klaviyo's pre-built templates for a cost-effective start, or hire a Klaviyo consultant for custom campaigns. Partner with a Klaviyo expert or a certified professional for seamless integration. The good news is that you can either learn these skills yourself or hire them at any budget. There are many professionals who are Klaviyo experts, and you can compare domestic prices and talent with low-cost overseas talent.

I want to be clear that the back-end setup for Yotpo is intense when you onboard with them. It takes about three months to set up, and you need a developer to work with them, or they won't even onboard you.

We pay our developers in India $2000 a month for unlimited ongoing web development. You can get a similarly skilled developer team for $500 a month or even $100 a month. We have had such a fantastic experience with our developers that we are happy to keep them on retainer since we are constantly building new pages and upgrading our website to support our SEO and marketing strategies. The cost is worth it to us. It would help if you considered hiring developers full-time because you can find them at any price level overseas.

Once you have lots of reviews coming in, it's important to note that customer reviews are some of the best sources of information on your business. They help you learn how to improve your products, make new products, and fix errors, leading to more sales. You may want to utilize tools like Monkey Learn's Review Analysis, which helps sift through all the review data and make sense of it to give you valuable insights. We like to rewrite our product listings and a lot of the language on our website based on customer reviews because they point to what people are searching for, which makes your website more relevant and helps your SEO.

Finally, if you want to consider using tools besides Yotpo, you can consider testing platforms like Bazaarvoice, which uses influencers to drive reviews and sales. It's always great to find and experiment with the latest tools that can streamline a marketing channel's workload or add AI capabilities to give you implementation speed above the competition.

Reviews are invaluable for establishing credibility and driving conversions, but cultivating them requires strategy and commitment. Start by collecting reviews through built-in or affordable solutions early, then level up to robust platforms like Yotpo as you grow. Integrate reviews with tools like Klaviyo to deliver personalized experiences. Though intensive to implement, the investment pays dividends through increased loyalty, recommendations, and sales. Fortunately, it's possible to automate, outsource, or hire professionals to manage the review process so you can focus on other marketing channels. With the proper foundation of reviews and seamless integrations, you can transform happy customers into a community of advocates who will explode your sales by rewarding your brand with their trust, voice, and business.

Resources from this chapter:

1. Yotpo: https://www.yotpo.com/

2. Trust Pilot: https://www.trustpilot.com/

3. Bazaarvoice:
https://www.bazaarvoice.com/products/always-on-content/

4. Monkey Learn's Review Analysis: https://monkeylearn.com/

Make a Difference with Your Review

Unlock the Power of Kindness

"A little thought and a little kindness are often worth more than
a great deal of money." - John Ruskin

Helping others without wanting anything back makes people happier and more successful. If we can spread some kindness together, I'm going to try.

I have a question for you...

Would you help someone you don't even know, even if they never find out it was you?

Who is this person? They are like you used to be. Still learning, wanting to make things better, and needing some help, but not sure where to look.

Our goal is to make ecommerce marketing easier for everyone. Everything I do comes from that goal. And the only way for me to achieve that is by reaching...well...everyone.

This is where you come in. Most people decide if a book is good or not by looking at the cover and reviews. So here is what I'm asking you to do to help someone struggling with ecommerce marketing that you've never met:

Please leave a review for this book.

Your kind act costs no money and takes less than 60 seconds, but it can change a fellow marketer's life forever. Your review could help...

...one more small business support their community....one more business owner provide for their family....one more employee get meaningful work....one more client transform their business.... make one more dream come true.

To get that warm feeling of helping someone and make a real difference, all you have to do is...it takes less than a minute...leave a review.

Just visit the link below or scan the QR code to leave your review:

https://www.amazon.com/review/review-your-purchases/?asin=B0D6QMH58T

If you feel good about helping a stranger, then you are my kind of person. Welcome to the club, one of us.

I'm even more excited to help you achieve mind-blowing ecommerce marketing success faster and more effectively than you ever thought possible. The game-changing tactics, eye-opening lessons, and cutting-edge AI-powered strategies I'll reveal in the coming chapters will blow you away.

Thank you from the bottom of my heart. Now, let's get back to our regularly scheduled programming.

— Your biggest fan, *Greg Pilla*

PS - Fun fact: If you provide value to someone, it makes you more valuable to them. If you'd like to pay it forward from one marketer to another - and you believe this book will help them - share this book.

Chapter 7

Influencer

We have yet to focus extensively on influencer marketing for our business, but we still have a plan to execute on it. Over the years, part of our hesitation stemmed from the notion that influencer marketing can resemble venture capital math – you might invest in numerous influencers, with only one yielding significant returns, while the vast majority fail to deliver.

Most influencers can be expensive, and you may not get anything out of working with them. However, the right influencer partnership can potentially drive a substantial influx of sales. It requires a dedicated team, budget, and patience.

To help justify the cost, you can repurpose the "user-generated content" from influencers for other marketing initiatives, such as advertisements. Traditionally, influencer marketing has been particularly helpful for companies aiming to drive app downloads, as a spike in downloads within a single day can propel an app to the top of app store charts, potentially leading to organic sales growth. While this strategy may be less relevant for ecommerce businesses, influencer marketing can still benefit SEO by driving increased traffic from diverse sources.

As you know, I strive to provide candid insights. Within our primary business, we haven't extensively engaged in influencer marketing over the years due to the concerns above. However, it's crucial to acknowledge that these apprehensions often stem from a non-strategic approach. A well-structured influencer marketing strategy, enhanced with AI tools, can yield a substantial return on investment.

When crafting an influencer marketing strategy, it's crucial to clearly understand your target audience and objectives. For instance, if you're a beauty brand, your ideal audience might encompass women aged 18 to 35 interested in vegan and cruelty-free cosmetics and actively follow beauty trends on social media platforms. Once you've defined your target demographic, establish specific goals, such as increasing conversions or generating leads, and tailor your influencer partnerships to align with those objectives. By having a well-defined target audience and articulated goals, you can effectively leverage influencer marketing to achieve your desired outcomes.

When selecting the right influencers for your campaign, it's advisable to consider micro-influencers with a following range of 1,000 to 100,000 individuals. These influencers are renowned for their high engagement rates within your niche or industry. Leveraging the appropriate tools can greatly assist you in identifying and vetting potential micro-influencers that align with your brand's values and target audience. By carefully curating a pool of relevant micro-influencers, you can effectively reach and resonate with your desired demographic, fostering meaningful connections and driving sales.

➡ AI PRO TIP You can leverage AI-powered tools to boost your influencer marketing. Upfluence, BuzzSumo, heepsy, AspireIQ, and emplifi.io are all great tools with some AI capabilities to check out. Consider Upfluence, which uncovers hidden gems – influencers who've already interacted with your brand but haven't been noticed. Heepsy, AspireIQ, and BuzzSumo are other great tools for finding and reaching out to influencers. BuzzSumo can predict the performance of potential influencer partnerships by analyzing historical data. As always, check out these tools and see what resonates with you or makes sense for you to test. The fantastic thing about these tools is they can manage most of the strategy and execution encompassing all of my recommendations in this chapter and put many of your influencer marketing functions on autopilot.

When it comes to influencer marketing, fostering genuine relationships is paramount. Seek partnerships with influencers who share your brand's values and have a vested interest in your success. You can cultivate authentic connections that pave the way for compelling and impactful content by aligning with like-minded individuals who resonate with your brand's ethos. These meaningful relationships, built on mutual understanding and shared goals, are the cornerstone of effective influencer marketing campaigns.

Establishing clear campaign briefs is essential for creating effective influencer marketing campaigns. These briefs should outline the goals, deliverables, guidelines, and creative direction while allowing influencers to inject their unique creativity. This ensures that the content resonates with their audience and aligns with your brand's ethos.

For instance, a campaign brief might include objectives such as increasing awareness and purchase intent for a new line of organic lipsticks while positioning your brand as a leader in clean, non-toxic beauty. The deliverables could encompass a sponsored Instagram feed post, an Instagram story unboxing and first impression, and a YouTube review video between 5-10 minutes.

Guidelines would specify showcasing 3-4 lipstick shades of the influencer's choosing, emphasizing the non-toxic ingredients and clean beauty positioning, and incorporating a promotional code for a discount on the first purchase. The creative direction may call for a bright, fresh, and natural aesthetic for photos and videos, focusing on lip swatches, texture close-ups, and authentic demonstrations of product benefits.

While providing this clear direction, it's crucial to encourage the influencer to select the exact products, design the shots, and inject their creativity into the narrative while communicating your core brand pillars. The goal is to balance providing clear expectations and allowing the influencer to authentically connect with their specific audience. By setting expectations while encouraging authenticity, you can foster the creation of great content that resonates with your target demographic and effectively conveys your brand's messaging.

Effective influencer marketing campaigns require robust tracking and optimization measures to ensure maximum impact and return on investment. Implement smart links using tools like Bitly or Google Campaign URL Builder to monitor the performance of influencer-generated content in real time. Leverage user-generated content (UGC) by encouraging influencers to initiate hashtag challenges that inspire their followers to create and share content. Tools like TINT can help curate and repurpose this UGC across various marketing platforms.

Moreover, amplify the reach of effective influencer content by sharing it through your brand's marketing channels and considering paid promotions for the most engaging posts. Diversify your influencer portfolio by collaborating with a mix of micro and macro-influencers, each with unique audience segments and strengths, to broaden your reach and appeal.

To thoroughly measure the ROI of your influencer marketing efforts, you could employ specific attribution modeling tools like "Impact" to trace direct and indirect sales back to influencer activities. These tools provide a precise measure of return on investment. As mentioned earlier, many of the tools can also assist with attribution tracking.

Once you identify successful tactics, replicate them with similar influencer profiles and expand the winning strategies across your campaigns. Encourage influencers to create content around specific keywords relevant to your products or services. For instance, if your product is a "sustainable yoga mat," have influencers create content that naturally includes this keyword, bolstering your brand's SEO efforts.

Ultimately, success doesn't lie in throwing money at random influencers but in smart strategy, data-driven insights, and cultivating genuine connections. With the right tools and approach, you can unlock the power of influencer marketing, connecting with your audience meaningfully and faster than ever before.

INFLUENCER BONUS SECTION: MINI CASE STUDY ON RALLY BIRD'S, PUNKLINGS

A good friend, Casey, who sells a stuffed animal called Punklings, experienced the viral potential of influencer marketing firsthand. When an influencer posted a raving video review, Casey received more orders in a single day than she had received in the entire previous year. Her Etsy store crashed, her website buckled, and backorders piled up for months. While this highlights the potential risks of rapid, unmanaged growth, it also showcases the remarkable power of influencer marketing to drive viral success. A single viral post can create an incredible surge in sales. However, you shouldn't treat influencer marketing as a lottery, hoping to hit the jackpot with a single campaign. Instead, consistent engagement with influencers raises the chances of eventually achieving viral success. With an intelligent influencer strategy, you, too, can capitalize on viral moments while sustaining consistent growth for your business.

Resources from this chapter:

1. Upfluence: https://upfluence.com/

2. Heepsy: https://www.heepsy.com/

3. AspireIQ: https://www.aspireiq.com/

4. emplifi.io: https://emplifi.io/

5. Bitly: https://bitly.com/

6. Google Campaign URL Builder: https://ga-dev-tools.appspot.com/campaign-url-builder/

7. TINT: https://www.tintup.com/

8. Impact: https://impact.com/

Chapter 8

Social Media Marketing

Entire books could be written about social media marketing alone, with each major platform like Facebook, Instagram, and TikTok warranting its own intricacies.

However, I will focus on simple, tactical strategies here.

First, realize that platforms like Facebook and Instagram limit organic reach to nudge brands towards paid promotion. However, there are still opportunities to expand reach through strategies like user-generated content.

Many companies find success in getting users to create engaging videos and then use that content in paid ads. This is where influencer marketing comes in - paying influencers to generate authentic, high-quality content.

The key is accepting the reality of paid social, while identifying creative ways to develop standout social content. User-generated influencer videos offer one promising avenue. With strategic planning, you can still break through the organic reach barriers.

Social media marketing involves more than just driving new customers through UGC, ads, and organic content. For our business, Instagram primarily facilitates community engagement.

For us, Instagram enables customers to easily find, learn about, and interact with our brand. These real-time interactions hold value, even if they don't directly generate sales. Customers appreciate having social access to brands, heightening loyalty and purchase intent.

Therefore, maintaining a social presence provides value, even if sales are not directly attributable. Consumers expect brands to be accessible on social channels nowadays. When a customer sends a direct message, they anticipate personalized responses.

View social platforms as communities to nurture, not just sales channels. The customer engagement and loyalty gained indirectly boosts purchasing over time. Deliver value through consistent interactions, not just promotional content.

➡AI PRO TIP I will let you in on the biggest game changer for next-level social media marketing - smart automation tools. There are excellent AI-powered options like RADAAR, Neulink, and Ocoya that can streamline managing your channels. Some consider RADAAR the most robust but explore all three to see which best fits your needs.

These tools integrate OpenAI's ChatGPT, and other plugins to execute social media tasks through a simple interface. For example, RADAAR enables the quick generation of social posts as images, text, or video and scheduling them across channels.

Creating and managing content used to take weeks of manual work, but AI-powered automation handles it in minutes. The main focus is simplifying your workflow and amplifying your social media impact through AI automation.

Strategic planning is critical to maximizing these tools. You can use the tool of your choice to map out content months ahead, with special emphasis on key shopping periods and holidays. When brands prepare well in advance, these seasonal events often spur sales surges.

These tools can automate much of the legwork in developing and creating content. However, continually hone your skills at producing engaging ideas or hire creative experts. For example, generate user content by challenging your audience to capture standout moments with your product. Dangle exciting prizes like new items or VIP experiences as incentives to participate.

The key is balancing automation with human creativity. Let the tools handle tedious tasks while focusing your energy on high-level strategy and innovative concepts. Combine smart software with human imagination, and you get the best of both worlds - efficient systems that enable clever ideas and immersive campaigns. Automate the busywork, but never stop pushing for that viral idea that ignites your audience.

Continuously pursuing growth is critical. Utilizing tools like RADAAR and consistent social strategies will drive organic development. Additionally, experiment across new platforms like Twitter using AI for content and engagement. Tools like tweethunter.io identify trending topics, enabling you to capitalize on viral momentum.

The key is a relentless growth mindset. Establish efficient foundations through core platforms like RADAAR. Then, expand your reach by tapping into additional networks and leveraging AI for optimized content. Stay on top of trending conversations and insert your brand seamlessly into relevant viral moments. With the right systems in place, you can rapidly test, react quickly, and maximize timely opportunities. Don't settle for the status quo - build adaptable processes to explore new channels and ride waves of attention.

To get started, choose platforms where your products naturally fit, such as Instagram for visuals or Twitter for quick updates, and plan your content strategy with tools like RADAAR to create and schedule posts. Engage your community and amplify your reach by leveraging user-generated content and influencer partnerships, utilizing platforms like AspireIQ and other tools mentioned in the influencer chapter for discovery and management. Adopting this approach will create a dynamic, data-driven social media presence that drives engagement and sales while keeping the process manageable and streamlined with the proper set of tools.

Resources from this chapter:

1. RADAAR: https://www.radaar.io/

2. Neulink: https://bit.ly/neulink1

3. Ocoya: https://bit.ly/ocoya3

4. tweethunter.io: https://tweethunter.io/

4. AspireIQ: https://www.aspireiq.com/

5. OpenAI (ChatGPT): https://www.openai.com/chatgpt

Chapter 9

Ads

For a few years, we did not run paid ads for TribeTokes. Operating in a highly regulated industry made it challenging, so we focused on other channels like SEO, where hard work could drive results without extra spending. However, as we matured and grew more strategic, we slowly introduced targeted ad campaigns to complement our marketing machine.

In the following few pages, I will give you a lot of recommendations and tools. As always, don't get overwhelmed. It's okay to take one recommendation or tool and test that for a few weeks. I want to give you a comprehensive overview of the Ad channel so you have all the tools and insights to (as always) move quickly on marketing tests.

Given its robust platform, most people look to Facebook first when considering paid ads. However, we learned Facebook ads only effectively work if your product costs over $50. The reason is the views and clicks come at too high a price, making it difficult to achieve a positive return on ad spend. The customer lifetime value (LTV) versus customer acquisition cost (CAC) ratio is very challenging for lower-priced products.

In other words, the amount you must pay per click or view on Facebook is higher than the revenue you can generate from low-priced products. You could end up spending more on the ad than you make back in sales. For example, if your product is $20 but costs you $15 to acquire a customer through Facebook ads, you lose money. The CAC is too high relative to the LTV.

However, we always recommend starting with Google AdWords first. When someone searches for your exact product or service, they have expressed clear buying intent. If you can't convert these highly targeted, low-funnel leads from Google, you will likely struggle to convert colder traffic from social media ads.

Therefore, before reading the rest of this chapter, you may want to stop and read a book or take a quick online course to master Google AdWords first to capture people who are actively looking to make a purchase. Once your high-intent funnel is optimized, expand into platforms like Facebook and Instagram to attract and retarget broader audiences. But begin by capitalizing on easy wins - people already searching for your offering. Prove your sales process works there before taking riskier shots down the funnel.

We previously discussed a highly effective strategy, which some call white-label social media ads, with influencers or creators. This involves having them generate authentic-looking third-party content featuring your product. You then amplify their posts through paid promotion, either from your ad account or through theirs, for maximum credibility.

In essence, it combines the power of influencer marketing with the targeting and reach of paid ads. Rather than pushing overtly branded creative, you spotlight organic creator content to capture attention. This leverages the strengths of both approaches - authenticity through influencers and scale through media buying. The synergy primes consumers through creators first, then retargets them with related ads for higher conversions.

The key is blending influencer content with strategic ad amplification for performance at scale. Instead of branded posts, put genuine third-party endorsements center stage and let your ad budget give them a boost.

I advised weighing the pros and cons of managing channels in-house versus hiring an agency. Many agencies have dedicated influencer and paid ad teams that can collaborate to execute this strategy. Their integrated capabilities and networks offer a crucial benefit for cross-channel amplification. More prominent brands may handle influencer partnerships and ad buying internally. However, most businesses leverage agencies to facilitate this synergistic approach.

With your expanded skills, you now have the know-how to execute everything yourself or outsource specific projects - giving you a significant competitive edge. You understand the whole picture and can make strategic decisions on handling influencer and ad coordination in-house or through an agency. This flexibility allows you to optimize your workflow, budgets, and results.

Let's discuss ad execution. Most think first of Google Ads, Facebook, and other social media ads, as well as programmatic display when it comes to digital advertising. You can think of each one as a potential channel to test. The issue with programmatic is poor attribution - any purchase from someone exposed to an ad gets attributed to it. However, many programmatic sales actually come from retargeting existing customers. People who visit your site will see your ads everywhere. Companies often wrongly assume those subsequent sales are due to the ads. In reality, other channels like email drove the initial site visit and purchase intent.

For example, an email promotion may have brought people to your site last week. They later bought after seeing your programmatic ad, but the purchase intent came from the email, not the display ad. With limited attribution data, it's easy to overestimate programmatic influence. Focus programmatic ads on retargeting to reinforce rather than claim full credit for cold conversions.

Programmatic agencies will sell you on brand awareness and being top of mind because when someone is browsing the internet, they are seeing your display ads everywhere, but it's not necessarily driving purchases. This is not to say don't do it, but exercise caution. It's like putting a billboard in Times Square - people will notice it, but it may not generate sales, so evaluate thoroughly before investing heavily.

The big problem with attribution, meaning not knowing whether or not an ad or another channel was the source of a sale, could be solved with sophisticated tools like Rockerbox. This tool is like a detective for your marketing efforts, examining the entire customer journey and determining which ads deserve the credit for that final sale. It's all about multi-touch attribution, so you'll see the whole story, not just the last chapter. While attributing sales and conversions to specific ads and campaigns is a common challenge faced by individual advertisers and even some agencies, you can leverage specialized tools to mitigate this risk and accurately track the performance of your advertising efforts. Using tools like Rockerbox is likely overkill for testing a channel. Initially, always keep your strategy and toolkit simple and add tools like Rockerbox as your team becomes more sophisticated.

If you want to narrow your focus, the most effective display ads for direct conversions are abandoned cart and browse retargeting. The Google program enabling this is called Dynamic Remarketing. It allows you to automatically show personalized ads to people who visited your site but didn't convert.

Here's how it works: A pixel is placed on your website to track browsing activity like product views and abandoned carts. (Remember you can hire a low-cost web developer or ad manager to help you implement programs like this) Leveraging the work of the pixel, Dynamic Remarketing generates customized ads featuring the specific products users engaged with but didn't purchase. These ads are then targeted to users across the Google Display Network as they browse other sites and apps.

By reminding users of the exact items they showed interest in, Dynamic Remarketing helps recapture their initial intent and nudge them to complete the purchase. Key features making this effective include automated ad creation from product feeds, hyper-personalized creative, scalable reach, and pay only for clicks.

Dynamic Remarketing powerfully reiterates your offering when motivation is highest, driving conversions through timely, individualized ads.

You have options when running ads. Larger brands commonly hire agencies, but self-serve platforms empower smaller teams to manage campaigns themselves. Tools like MediaMath and GumGum optimize targeting and placement. MediaMath maximizes your budget, while GumGum ensures contextual relevance. Another tool called Adacado, as their site states, lets you "make personalized ads on the fly" quickly.

The benefit is the ability to experiment with in-house management. By learning and testing one or two of these platforms, you can take the reins and compare them to outsourcing. Platforms like Adroll cater to smaller teams and budgets. As their site says, Adroll works for "one-person marketing" and "marketing newbies" with "smaller budgets needing smarter dollars." The message is clear - the right tools allow even modest businesses to self-manage ad campaigns.

The key is flexibility. You now have viable self-service options to test beyond just agencies. Take time to evaluate which approach optimizes your resources. The skills to leverage tools like Adacado and Adroll equip you to find the right balance of in-house and outsourced expertise.

You can get super creative when creating ads yourself, but you don't have to. Start simple. To Craft a compelling Ad journey, create ads that showcase a problem your audience cares about. Then, introduce your product as the solution, and finally, hit them with a strong call to action. If you're marketing eco-friendly water bottles, begin with the impact of single-use plastics on the environment, followed by how your bottles offer a solution, and conclude with a tempting offer to make that first purchase.

Don't get me wrong - outsourcing to experts is often advisable to scale fast. However, having the option to test in-house allows comparison to determine the right long-term mix. The goal is to equip you with the tools and knowledge to evaluate running some or all media internally if desired. With the right platforms, even small teams can optimize ad campaigns themselves. So don't think agencies are the only route - ad technology empowers companies of all sizes to take the reins.

Experimenting with paid ads is a game of finding a strategy and process that truly works. Eventually, you or an agency you hire may find a channel where you can spend $10 and make back $20. You can then keep scaling that profitable ad channel to spur significant business growth.

At that point, many businesses run into the difficult task of ensuring sufficient cash flow to keep up with accelerating ad and inventory spending. In an ideal world, the ads' profits would fuel this growth. However, issues like inventory lag times often force companies to borrow money to feed the ad engine.

Be extremely careful when taking on debt, as it could crush your business if a campaign suddenly underperforms. At the same time, take calculated risks to scale effective channels, as you are smart enough to do this prudently when laser-focused on proven profitability. While others may spend just where they see growth, you will spend where actual profits are generated.

<u>Resources from this chapter:</u>

1. Google AdWords: https://ads.google.com/

2. Rockerbox: https://rockerbox.com/

3. MediaMath: https://www.mediamath.com/

4. GumGum: https://gumgum.com/

5. Adacado: https://adacado.com/

6. Adroll: https://www.adroll.com/

Chapter 10

Reddit

The Reddit community is highly engaged, so if you can target a community relevant to your company, you can potentially achieve excellent results.

Advertising on Reddit tends to be expensive, so proceed cautiously.

The good thing about Reddit is that they assign you a representative to help you develop and launch your ads so you can do it yourself without necessarily having an agency.

Advertising on Reddit can be a highly effective way to reach engaged communities, each centered around a subreddit. With a user base that values genuine connections and content, targeted advertising on this platform can yield substantial engagement and conversions.

Research and target relevant subreddits. Do a deep dive by spending some time on Reddit to understand the culture of subreddits that align with your brand. If your product is eco-friendly water bottles, look beyond the obvious choices like "environment." Delve into lifestyle subreddits such as camping gear or zero waste, where discussions about sustainability may naturally occur.

Implement tracking pixels to attribute conversions from Reddit ads back to your website or other channels. This clarity helps optimize budget allocation across platforms. Popular analytic tools like Google Analytics, Adobe Analytics, and Mixpanel can incorporate Reddit data.

For ad targeting, you can leverage Reddit's search function and look at the subreddit's size, engagement level, and relevance to your niche. Subreddits with highly active daily users and posts receiving substantial upvotes indicate an active community. Utilize Reddit's advertising platform to direct your ads to these vibrant subreddits.

Consider using promoted posts to organically seed your content vs. traditional ads. Promoted posts look and feel just like native Reddit content. For example, you could create a post showcasing customers using your reusable bottles while hiking and promote that to outdoor subreddits. This authentically engages communities where your brand fits.

➡ AI PRO TIP Create authentic and value-driven content. Your content should align with the unique interests of each subreddit community, like sharing testimonials of individuals using your bottles in outdoor settings. Engage AI writing assistants like Claude, Gemini, or Chat GPT to draft ad copy that feels native to Reddit users. Authenticity is critical; hard-sell tactics are often met with resistance.

Test different ad formats beyond text/image posts. Video and carousel ads can stand out and have higher engagement in some communities. Measure performance to guide creative.

It's essential to engage with the community as an active participant. Go beyond advertising by participating in subreddit discussions to demonstrate your commitment to the community. Use community engagement as a feedback mechanism. For instance, if users discuss the importance of BPA-free products, use this opportunity to highlight these features in your product line and consider this input for future product development.

I highly recommend utilizing Reddit's Ad Support team. Reddit's ad support is exceptional. It provides advertisers with dedicated account managers to guide them through the advertising process, an advantage not commonly offered by all platforms. These representatives help you understand best practices and optimize your campaigns for the Reddit audience.

As you continue with this marketing channel test, closely monitor and optimize your Ads. Track the performance of your campaigns with Reddit's native analytics tools. Monitor Reddit comments and user feedback closely. Sentiment analysis tools like Awario.com or Hootsuite.com can automate this process. Address concerns transparently.

Balance organic and paid strategies. Develop a genuine organic presence by regularly contributing valuable content and insights. Use paid ads to supplement your organic approach, especially highlighting new products or promotions.

To scale up your organic Reddit activity, create a content calendar that aligns with major events or discussions happening within your targeted subreddits. If you can staff someone on this project, have someone dedicated to engaging with the community, responding to comments, creating posts about relevant topics, and sharing user-generated content that showcases your brand's impact.

Consider leveraging Reddit influencers or creators to organically showcase your brand to their engaged following. Find good brand fits through relevant subreddits.

In summary, when done thoughtfully, Reddit offers distinctive opportunities to connect with highly engaged communities. Take time to research the culture and interests of relevant subreddits. Create content that provides authentic value vs. pure promotion. Engage organically by contributing to discussions. Leverage Reddit's self-serve ad platform to complement organic efforts. Track performance closely and optimize based on data and user feedback.

Brands can build a strong Reddit presence with the right strategic balance of paid and organic activity, tailored creative, and active community participation. Don't be afraid to test Reddit quickly to validate if it aligns with your goals. Run small pilot campaigns to gauge potential before investing heavily. Those finding product-channel fit can then scale efforts while preserving the Reddit ethos. In a platform valuing authenticity, simply "showing up" isn't enough - you must show up authentically. But first, show up through testing to see if the channel works for you.

<u>Resources from this chapter:</u>

1. Google Analytics: https://analytics.google.com/

2. Adobe Analytics:
https://www.adobe.com/analytics/analytics-cloud.html

3. Mixpanel: https://mixpanel.com/

4. Awario: https://awario.com/

5. Hootsuite: https://www.hootsuite.com/

6. Claude: https://www.anthropic.com

7. Gemini: https://gemini.google.com/

Chapter 11

Charles Peralo Case Study

Before delving into a specific plan for executing a YouTube marketing and advertising channel, I want to share a case study on a YouTube's success story. My friend Charles Peralo is among the most successful people I know on YouTube and TikTok. While Charles doesn't have an ecommerce business and grows his YouTube channel for his own reasons, many lessons can be learned from his approach and how he executes growing a channel.

Charles essentially posts about trendy topics in the news, often conducting extensive research (usually financial) to create videos on interesting, trendy subjects. For instance, he might explore "How did Ryan Reynolds make $340 million from the sale of Mint Mobile?" More importantly, Charles utilizes the key lesson of rapid iteration. He has a niche of commenting on trendy or celebrity topics with a unique spin, but he constantly improves and iterates within YouTube and TikTok to increase his reach.

The reason I want to share excerpts from my conversation with Charles is to provide insights into organic growth approaches beyond SEO. While a significant portion of this book deals with paid advertising channels outside of cmail markcting and SEO, it's also important to highlight how you can grow a platform without advertising. You can develop a substantial following on platforms like Instagram, YouTube, and TikTok and then drive that audience to your products or services.

First, here is a paraphrased version of Charles' Facebook Post (March 2023) in Charles' own words

In 2010, I got really into YouTube and said I wanted to make content there. I tried it, but it didn't hit. I deleted all the content, and for 12 years, I kept saying I wanted to try it again one day.

I got active on TikTok in January 2021 and ignored YouTube all of 2021, not believing in YouTube Shorts or reposting content as a realistic way to grow a channel. I only began reposting when my friend Neil started yelling at me on every call, saying it would work, and I was letting a few dud videos on YouTube get to me.

I started getting active on YouTube, reposting my videos in January 2022. By February, my videos were going viral, averaging over 1 million daily views. Last night, I hit a new milestone: 500,000 subscribers, 609,000,000 total views, and 991 videos on YouTube, with an average of 614,000 views each.

YouTube has been an amazing experience. It took 12 years to go from 0 to 500 subscribers, with mainly procrastinating, but it took only one year to go from 0 to 500,000 subscribers. Now, I'm on a path where I expect to hit the billion view mark by October/November of 2023.

Let me dive into what I'm up to and the future I see for my channel. There are really three parts to how I got here:

YouTube Shorts

These are just reposts of videos I make on TikTok, which amazingly does better on YouTube than TikTok. I currently average about 1.5 million views per day, with some months around 2 million, just on YouTube. I prefer the YouTube algorithm to TikTok's because of how it works.

TikTok is very much about the auto-viral factor. I've posted videos there and often had 1-5 million views in 24 hours. YouTube doesn't work like that. Videos normally go viral 10, 20, 30, and even 60 days after posting. I'm also seeing a resurge effect now, where popular videos from a year ago are gaining

1-3 million new views over 30-45 days on the year anniversary of posting. That doesn't happen on TikTok.

Why are my videos successful? I focus on the celebrity niche, which shocks most people who know me, but I've always loved the entertainment business. I've found a niche where I make pop culture a bit smarter. It's honestly kind of cool. I'll find a headline like Holly Madison saying she didn't take birth control when with Hugh Hefner, and I turn that into a 1-minute video on the science of men having kids at an older age. Boom, a million views! That happens a lot, and sometimes I laugh at the videos, but I often love how they go viral and put some solid information out there. I don't think this trend will slow down, and I think I'll have 5-10 billion views or more from this niche by 2030.

Polls

A lot of YouTubers know me as the polls guy, and I'll take the title of the best person doing that. This started on Facebook for me. I saw YouTube allows that function, and it now averages about 1.5 million votes per day. Many voters say they've never seen my videos.

What's remarkable is that I just started doing image polls and, before, always had an "unsure" option. Now I put myself as the unsure option, so my face gets seen by over a million people per day with little actual work.

My polls work because I find big questions most people don't normally think about, which are much better than the standard "Who'd win, Iron Man or Thor" questions, which are awful.

Posts

I love writing and researching, which began as a hobby during the pandemic. I began posting everything there, where I have thousands of daily readers, many of whom tell me they like that content more than anything else.

I also get personal sometimes. After my dad passed away, my post about him got over 47,000 likes, and 200,000+ people saw it. Many felt they got to know me better.

It's also great for spitballing ideas, where I'll pitch comic/movie plots, businesses I want to start, and so on. My gut feeling is that the YouTube community page is the future of blog culture. I've built an active audience on it, and I believe when I launch Peralo.com, I'll hit 25,000+ email subscribers.

And finally, what's next?

The big thing is long-form content, and I'm still really mixed on it, so I think I'll try a hybrid of ideas until finding the one that really works.

Idea One: Dhar Mann-type videos

While I can't say I love YouTuber Dhar Mann's content or management, he's amazing in how he's found a way to create low-budget scripted content. For under $1,000, he has videos reaching tens of millions.

YouTube is very much a reality TV platform now, but this guy's approach to scripted content is, in my opinion, the future. I've recently made plans with editors, camera guys, and actors to begin producing 8-minute scripted videos, which will be me and friends of mine, writing, acting, and directing. The goal is something I'd want to view, like the Twilight Zone meets Dhar Mann.

It's a massive jump from what I currently do, but I don't think it'll be a big deal. A lot of YouTubers do things such as music videos, which are heavily out of niche, and I'll still be in the videos, which works.

The real reason is that I've had a passion for writing fiction for years, with a goal to make movie franchises eventually. This seems like a path for it, and one I'm probably more passionate about than any other content.

Idea Two: Fitness meets Binging with Babish

One of my favorite YouTubers and easily the best food YouTuber is Binging with Babish, who does food videos based on movies/shows. This is what I call the Remora Effect, which is creators doing their field but circling a big fish.

I am pretty active in fitness, and while others are trying it, nobody seems to be doing solid fitness content, where something like "Brad Pitt fight club abs" is a thing and does it in a solid video. This could have strong subscriber retention, but I am mixed if it caps me too much in that niche.

Idea Three: Mr. Beast, but educational

I've been solid at writing on a wide range of topics and incorporating solid data into them. I get asked all the time why I don't make them videos, and the reason is just the views wouldn't be there.

I'd have to do something very big and make it educational to do that.

Some examples:

Did Ray Kroc actually steal McDonald's? Becomes "Buying 1,000 McDonald's Cheeseburgers."

Was the Oreo a ripoff? Becomes "Making the world's largest Oreo."

Why is dental so expensive? Becomes, "I fixed this guy's teeth."

The model would be finding a heavily viral title, doing something very cool, creating a video around that, and layering on real data, turning it educational. I have a directorial style in mind for that, but I'm still mixed on how to execute it. The issue is obviously cost, as I'm not 100% sold it'd warrant it. This will likely happen, but probably not for a little while.

Final thoughts:

YouTube is one of the coolest experiences of my life. It's surreal that, through YouTube, TikTok, Snapchat, and other places, I reach several million people a day.

However, YouTube is the one I'm most excited about for the future. I feel that in 3-10 years, I could be one of the largest people on the platform, with 5-10 billion views and 10+ million subscribers.

It took 12 years to get the nerve to start uploading and see what happened in a single year. I won't wait another decade for any goals here or any of my other goals.

Next, I interviewed Charles to gain deeper insights into the concepts outlined in the above post and learn more about the evolution of his business, gleaning fascinating takeaways from his responses, which are paraphrased in his own words:

First up, it's a cool milestone that I'm almost at a million subscribers now. I've learned that YouTube is a game of different algorithms, where shorts, community posts, and regular videos all play by different rules. Succeeding in one format doesn't guarantee success in another.

I recently made these two videos—"Was McDonald's Stolen?" and "Dan Schneider is a creep," respectively —but they're just not landing how I'd hoped. Compare that to my shorts, which average over 500,000 views, and my polls/quizzes, which get 2 million daily voters. It's wild how different the performance can be across formats.

As for traditional long-form YouTube revenue, I'm doing 8-12 minute videos with around 45% watch time, averaging 35,000-40,000 views. The revenue I'm seeing off those views is $170-220. There's this gap between CPM and RPM, too. CPM might suggest $370 in revenue, but RPM, which is what's actually paid out, is around $180. Do the math, and 100,000 views is like $430; a million is $4,300. It doesn't sound like much, but scale that up to 2 million monthly views, and we're talking about almost $100K a year just from YouTube.

But sponsorships really kick things up a notch. I recently landed my first long-form sponsor deal at $450 per video with a 30,000-view minimum. That's a $15 CPM, which is actually on the lower end - the market norm is more like $20-25 CPM. If I could average 200,000 views, I could charge $4,000 per sponsored video. Do four of those a month, and we're looking at $16,000 in sponsor money alone, not counting the $4,000 or so from YouTube's cut. Nearly $20K monthly from 200K views isn't bad!

Then, with YouTube Shorts, they pay differently based on length. I use the full minute and make around $200 a day off 40 million monthly Shorts views.

But the real engagement goldmine is my community page - 1.9 billion impressions in 2023 alone and over 200,000 new subscribers, all from polls and quizzes that take me 20-30 minutes per day to create. That kind of reach is invaluable for building a brand.

Now, Shorts don't pay amazingly; one recent video with 1 million views only paid out about $140 after the delay. It shows that you could get 100 million Shorts views and only make $15-20K. But I'm putting 2-3 hours into the Shorts each day across YouTube, and TikTok is netting me around $10K per month and $120K annually. Not too shabby for less than part-time work!

I've also done about $25K from sponsored Shorts, but that market feels like it's dying down a bit. The real focus is growing the long-form - if those videos start popping off, hoo boy. Look at Phillip DeFranco pulling $10-20K sponsors per video. We're talking $100K-250K monthly channel revenue potential.

My goal is to create these long-form hybrid news/mini-documentary-style videos. I've also had great success with Snapchat Shows, which require special approval. I currently have three approved and a deal in the works to take over 11 more Series in the near future. These limited-run premium shows can be huge moneymakers - I've personally had Snap Show episodes clear six-figures.

To give you an idea, here are the pilots for two of my Snap Shows that I uploaded to YouTube: "Mosquitoes Kill Millions" and "Back to the Future Sued for Millions." Usually, they're narrated, but pilots have me on camera. The Jenna Ortega episode did over $100K in revenue alone!

Moving forward, I really want to reinvent the written article format with Peralo.com. People are bored with just straight articles and books. I want to build out interactive articles with embedded quizzes, polls, you name it - gamify the whole experience of learning about a topic.

These quizzes I'm making are getting hundreds of thousands of daily readers already, so the engagement is there. Combining that with AI to customize content complexity for each individual's existing knowledge... that's the future of educational content.

My vision for Peralo.com is to use quizzes as an intuitive, interactive gateway into articles and fundamentally change how we learn online. No more just reading a dry article - it's going to be a full, hands-on, self-guided exploration. Almost like those old classic Xbox games that were part game, part interactive experience alongside the story, you know?

Overall Takeaway

While Charles Peralo doesn't operate an eCommerce business directly, his innovative approach to content creation and audience building offers valuable insights that can be adapted to drive sales for ecommerce brands. Like Charles, who succeeded in the celebrity/pop culture niche, ecommerce businesses should identify their target audience and create content that resonates with them. The content could involve exploring trending topics, addressing common pain points, or showcasing products in unique ways that capture attention and provide value.

A key lesson from Charles' success is the importance of rapid iteration, experimentation, and diversifying content offerings. To maximize reach and engagement, he constantly iterates and improves his content across different formats like shorts, polls, and long-form videos. Similarly, ecommerce businesses should continuously test, refine, and diversify their content strategies based on data and audience feedback. The strategic feedback loop could involve creating a varied mix of content such as product tutorials, behind-the-scenes glimpses, user-generated content, immersive shopping experiences, and leveraging short and long-form formats. A diverse, ever-evolving content portfolio optimized through experimentation is crucial for driving engagement and growth.

Fostering a sense of community and engagement has been pivotal for Charles. He has built a highly engaged community through interactive polls, personal storytelling, and idea-sharing. Ecommerce businesses can cultivate a similar sense of community by encouraging user-generated content, facilitating discussions, and fostering genuine connections with their audience.

Charles's proposed startup for creator monetization demonstrates the importance of innovative revenue streams. To complement their core product sales, ecommerce businesses can explore alternative monetization strategies, such as affiliate marketing, influencer collaborations, or subscription-based models.

Finally, staying agile and adaptable is critical in the ever-evolving digital landscape. Charles's willingness to adapt and embrace new trends has been instrumental to his success. Ecommerce businesses must remain agile and closely monitor emerging platforms, technologies, and consumer behaviors to stay ahead of the curve.

By applying these lessons from Charles's case study, ecommerce businesses can build a loyal following and drive targeted traffic and sales through engaging content, community-building efforts, and innovative monetization strategies. Continuously experimenting, iterating, and adapting will be crucial for long-term success in the dynamic ecommerce arena.

Chapter 12

Youtube

In the previous chapter, there were many valuable lessons embedded in Charles Peralo's story as one of the top content creators on YouTube, particularly strategies for growing a channel organically. This follow-up chapter focuses on traditional YouTube marketing and advertising strategies if you decide to pursue YouTube as a channel to test and grow to drive sales. However, if you choose to build a channel organically like Charles, that could yield immense results.

What we like about YouTube videos is that they are somewhat evergreen. Unlike many social media platforms where content quickly gets lost in the feed once it falls out of view, YouTube is searchable, making it an ideal platform for evergreen content such as HOW-TOs or PRODUCT REVIEWS. However, you might not achieve that initial virality.

In the ever-changing ecommerce marketing landscape, the ability to adapt is crucial. A strategic blend of evergreen content and trending topics is crucial for cultivating a dynamic YouTube presence that resonates with your audience. This balanced approach empowers you to capitalize on viral trends while simultaneously building a timeless content repository, consistently attracting viewers and driving sales over time.

To rapidly build a powerful YouTube presence, establish ambitious yet achievable objectives from the outset. For businesses already active on the platform, aim for month-over-month growth that steadily increases your channel views and subscriber count. The primary focus should be on optimizing your content and strategy to convert an ever-increasing proportion of viewers into paying customers. If you're new to YouTube, set your sights on consistent viewership growth as you lay the foundation for your channel's eventual dominance. Consistently push for accelerated expansion and viewer engagement right from the start.

Conduct a thorough analysis of your audience's search behaviors and preferences using AI-powered tools like TubeBuddy or VidIQ. These keyword research tools can optimize video titles, descriptions, and tags for enhanced SEO and visibility. For instance, if your business specializes in eco-friendly products, tailor your content to highlight sustainability practices, DIY recycling tutorials, or the impact of single-use plastics, directly addressing the environmental concerns of your target demographic.

➡ AI PRO TIP When crafting dynamic videos, explore cutting-edge AI creation tools to find the right fit for your needs and workflow. Tools like Runway, Fliki, and invideo.io effortlessly generate engaging ideas and content. Runway transforms text prompts into captivating visuals, while Fliki offers pre-made templates optimized for platforms like YouTube. Invideo.io provides an end-to-end AI-powered solution. Test these tools to discover which resonates best with your creative process for video content.

If you're filming your own videos, consider using a tool like Descript to streamline the editing process. Descript generates transcripts of your videos, allowing you to edit the text and seamlessly alter the corresponding video. Additionally, it enables you to incorporate stock footage seamlessly, enhancing the quality and appeal of your content.

If you're new to this area, consider hiring an agency or freelancer to help implement your YouTube advertising strategy, at least initially. You can also learn the platform yourself by leveraging Google's Ads Academy courses and guides. With some upfront learning, Google Ads is quite manageable for driving your own YouTube ad campaigns.

To drive immediate sales, leverage In-Stream Ads through the Google Ads platform. These are the short video ads that play before a viewer's chosen YouTube content. Use the video creation tools mentioned earlier to craft attention-grabbing 5-15 second ads highlighting promotions or new products to make a strong first impression.

To complement in-stream ads, set up Discovery Ads which appear on YouTube homepages, search results, and related videos sections. Utilize longer videos, up to 2 minutes, engagingly showcasing your products/services to encourage viewers to visit your site.

Implement a balanced strategy utilizing both In-Stream Ads for immediate sales impact and Discovery Ads for sustained nurturing. Create a content plan, produce ads using intuitive video makers, set up the campaigns in Google Ads, and continually optimize based on data to maximize sales.

While YouTube advertising directly reaches your target audience, influencer marketing allows you to tap into engaged communities. Leverage the earlier influencer strategies by utilizing tools like Upfluence, BuzzSumo, heepsy, or AspireIQ to identify suitable influencers. Then, use Repurpose.io to transform your marketing videos into optimized content for the influencers' preferred platforms to expand your global reach.

Repurpose.io's multi-platform publishing capabilities enable you to simultaneously implement your YouTube ad campaigns while distributing influencer content across multiple channels like TikTok, Instagram, Facebook, and more. This strategic combination of paid advertising and influencer marketing covers all the bases to drive sales from both new and existing audiences.

For a seamless ecommerce integration, create shoppable videos by embedding direct product page links using YouTube's "Cards" and "End Screens" features. Cards appear within the video player, while End Screens showcase towards the end, allowing viewers to seamlessly visit your site and make purchases after watching. This powerful functionality can significantly boost engagement and conversions from your video marketing efforts by providing a frictionless shopping experience. Test shoppable elements across the various video creation platforms to unlock this revenue-driving potential.

In the ever-evolving landscape of ecommerce marketing, harnessing the power of YouTube is paramount. By setting measurable objectives, leveraging AI tools for audience analysis and content creation, implementing a strategic advertising approach, collaborating with influencers, repurposing content across channels, and integrating shoppable links, you can cultivate a robust YouTube presence that bolsters your ecommerce endeavors, driving sustainable business growth.

Resources from this chapter:

1. Invideo.io: Retrieved from https://bit.ly/invideo5

2. Repurpose.io: https://bit.ly/repurpose5

3. Descript: https://www.descript.com/

4. Google Ads Academy: https://ads.google.com/home/resources/

5. TubeBuddy: https://www.tubebuddy.com/

6. VidIQ: https://vidiq.com/AIECOMM

7. Runway: https://runwayml.com/

8. Fliki: https://bit.ly/Fliki3

Chapter 13

TikTok

Before delving into TikTok marketing strategies, let's explore insights from Charles Peralo's experience building a successful presence on the platform. His journey sheds light on the nuances of the TikTok algorithm compared to YouTube, offering valuable lessons that could inform an effective content approach for achieving organic growth on TikTok. Here is an excerpt from Charles in his own words:

I'm really happy to hit a new milestone on TikTok, getting my 100 millionth likes last night. So I wanted to do a quick breakdown of the last year for me on TikTok - how the content is going, where I see this app evolving, and how this 100 million number is, in some ways, a bad thing for me.

First, the bad news. While I've amassed over 100 million likes and 750 million total views on TikTok, my follower-to-like ratio isn't great. In fact, out of accounts that have reached the 100 million like mark, I'd be shocked if even ten didn't have at least a million followers, which I don't at just 600,000.

The issue seems to stem partially from my niche of providing breakdowns on pop culture and entertainment topics, which doesn't naturally lend itself to gaining a large following. Also, I don't infuse a ton of personality into my content. While I occasionally add jokes, I typically keep the main focus on objectively covering the subject matter rather than making it about myself. These factors likely contribute to my follower count lagging behind the number of likes and overall views.

I was told to say, "Please follow," but I've done that, and it hasn't made any negligible change in retention. This is an issue because there are accounts with 5-20 times my current follower count that have fewer likes/views.

But look, I've reached that milestone across social media of over a billion views and a million followers combined, so this follower-to-like ratio issue on TikTok is simply a new puzzle for me to crack!

Now, back to the good stuff though. Let's talk about TikTok as a whole. I'm active on both TikTok and YouTube, where I've had over half a billion views on YouTube and almost 500,000 subscribers there. The content is EXACTLY the same, with me doing YouTube Shorts from reposted TikTok videos.

Same content, but the two places have different algorithms. YouTube's algorithm is different in two ways.

The first is that YouTube wants creators to post a lot of content, and I've seen view drops during months when I posted less, not even for a general sense, but in individual videos. My gut feeling is that they do this to avoid YouTube becoming like TikTok, where people randomly go viral and gain followers. It's more of a process.

The second is that YouTube views are rarely gained quickly. Over 150 videos have broken a million views on YouTube, but only one hit over 1 million in under 48 hours, and my most viral videos typically gain views over months. Hell, one video posted a year ago just randomly gained 500,000+ views in the last week.

TikTok doesn't do that. A video I posted last week got 5 million views in just three days, but it didn't grow much after that.

My feeling on this is that TikTok wants people to have that auto-success feeling of going viral, whereas YouTube only wants to work with more dedicated creators.

Neither platform is right or wrong, but both have pros and cons. I do prefer YouTube, though!"

Organic TikTok marketing is exploding, creating massive opportunities for ecommerce brands to tap into this dynamic platform and connect with potential customers. However, as savvy creators like Charles Parello have learned, succeeding on TikTok requires a nuanced, multi-faceted strategy that aligns with the platform's unique style, trends, and youth-driven audience.

While TikTok's popularity is soaring, you'll want to evaluate whether the platform aligns with your brand personality and product offering. As Charles found, TikTok's fun, playful atmosphere may not be an ideal fit for every brand, given that his entertainment/pop culture niche content saw success but struggled to convert into follows. However, if your products have highly visual features that can be showcased engagingly in short videos, you're likely well-suited for TikTok success. Social listening tools like Brandwatch or Talkwalker can help gauge existing conversations around your brand niche on the platform.

After confirming TikTok is a viable channel, create a straightforward content calendar. Research popular trends, challenges, holidays, and cultural moments that align with your audience's interests. For example, Google Trends or TikTok's own Trending section can be used to identify topics and hashtags that are gaining traction. Then, brainstorm ways to incorporate those trends into your content in an authentic, on-brand way. Be selective in choosing trends that complement your brand.

➡ AI PRO TIP For example, use an AI video creation tool like InVideo to superimpose your product on a background featuring a viral TikTok dance or challenge. Or create a duet-style video that intercuts your product demo with reaction clips of an influencer or customer experiencing the product for the first time, alongside footage of another currently viral TikTok trend or meme. For instance, a beverage brand could duet the "Corn Kid" viral clip by showing someone trying their latest drink flavor, spliced with the kid's enthusiastic "It's so good!" reaction. The key is identifying ways to promote your offerings through on-trend videos instead of forcing overt ads.

Consistently analyze the tones, subject matter, and content formats that resonate with your audience based on analytics from TikTok's Creator Tools. Use that data to guide the styles and trends you use to create automated videos.

If you sell kitchen gadgets, repurpose a top food influencer's viral recipe video by blending in clips showcasing how your product could be used. Or create montage videos capitalizing on trending hashtags like #TikTokMadeMeBuyIt to promote impulse purchases.

The video creation tools let you nimbly experiment by quickly producing on-trend content matched to your audience's interests without major filming requirements. Using an AI content calendar, you can stick to a consistent posting cadence to build long-term momentum cost-effectively.

To streamline the content creation process while ensuring high quality, start experimenting with AI video editing platforms like invideo.io. This cutting-edge tool harnesses advanced machine learning capabilities to automatically generate polished video clips simply from the text prompts you provide. For example, you could describe a concept to invideo's AI like "an unboxing video for a new skincare product line with a tropical vibe," and it will produce a complete draft video that you can then tweak and customize to infuse your specific branding and messaging. The AI leverages techniques like text-to-speech, background removal, and intelligent video editing to create videos at scale.

As you're developing a content strategy, take full advantage of TikTok's built-in ecommerce tools and shopping features designed to drive sales. The TikTok Shopping suite allows you to add product links and catalog integration, so viewers can seamlessly purchase items directly through your TikTok videos with just a couple of taps. Branded hashtag challenges are another powerful approach. A fitness apparel company could launch the #FitFashionChallenge, asking TikTok users to show off how they rock the brand's latest athletic looks.

Another powerful approach is to run TikTok's "Branded Mission" ad units, which incentivize users to create and share branded video content through a sponsored challenge. To launch a Branded Mission, you'll first create a launch video ad that explains the challenge prompt and prize details. For example, a clothing company could offer $500 cash prizes to the top 10 TikTokers who film the most creative videos showing how they styled outfits using the brand's new collection. This taps into the viral, user-generated content that TikTok's community loves.

While cultivating a robust organic presence is paramount, drawing from strategies employed by savvy creators like Charles, incorporating paid advertising should also be a key part of your TikTok marketing mix. TikTok's advertising capabilities utilize advanced AI and machine learning models to enable incredibly precise audience targeting based on parameters like interests, behaviors, job titles, locations, past engagement patterns, and even real-world foot traffic data. You can finely define your ideal customer right down to the smallest details.

When producing your TikTok video ads, turn again to AI-powered tools like invideo.io that offer unique editing capabilities to generate scroll-stopping creatives efficiently at scale. Their Smart Edit feature uses AI to automatically create variations with different hooks, calls-to-action, and product features spotlighted, saving you from manually recreating numerous ad versions.

As your organic and paid TikTok campaigns start rolling out, it's critical to closely monitor performance analytics at every stage using TikTok's comprehensive reporting suite. Track your core metrics such as video views, engagement rates (including comments and shares), click-through rates, website traffic sources, and audience demographics. Having this detailed data is critical to effectively optimizing your TikTok strategy.

To truly understand which videos directly impact purchases, set up the TikTok Pixel and integrate your ecommerce store data. The TikTok Pixel is a tracking code that allows you to view corresponding website actions like purchases, add-to-carts, checkouts initiated, and more for each TikTok video view. Connecting this purchase data through the Pixel closes the attribution loop.

With this integrated data, TikTok Ads Manager's AI-powered trend analysis can identify patterns in the content themes, creative approaches, messaging angles, and product demonstrations that resonate most strongly with your audiences based on trackable actions like purchases and add-to-carts. Using machine learning models, the AI can surface insights like your top-performing hashtags, video lengths, product focus areas, and more.

For brands with the resources to run more advanced optimization, leveraging A/B testing can take your TikTok performance to the next level. If you have the bandwidth, here's how you could implement a data-driven testing approach:

Utilize an AI video generation tool like Invideo to rapidly produce multiple creative variations. It can automatically generate videos with different hooks, product features spotlighted, aspect ratios, lengths, and more. Simply input your guidelines and sample assets.

Next, upload these variations into TikTok Ads Manager as draft ads. TikTok's AI will allow you to create a streamlined A/B test, deploying the different video ads to similar test audience segments. As the videos run, you can view granular performance metrics like view-through rates, clicks, and conversions for each variation.

The A/B tests provide valuable data illuminating which specific creative concepts are driving the best results with your target customers. You can then model future organic and paid video content after the top-performing hooks, product demos, and video specs that proved most engaging and motivating. Regularly refreshing your creatives based on what quantifiably works best allows for continuous optimization.

Recreate your highest-converting TikTok videos as ads tailored to custom audiences built with TikTok Ads Manager's AI prospecting tools. Use TikTok's integrated Spark Ads creator to seamlessly transform your top organic videos into shoppable ad units with clickable product pins and checkout integrations to maximize sales directly from your videos.

Successfully marketing your ecommerce brand on TikTok boils down to a few key elements executed consistently. First, set clear objectives for priority metrics like website visitors, sales revenue, and customer acquisition cost. Use a tool like TikTok Analytics to benchmark and track your goals. Then, study your target audiences' interests, content preferences, and purchasing behavior using TikTok's insights tools (Audience Integration allows you to import and analyze your customer data) to create content tailored to what resonates with them.

Don't overthink it - model your style and vibe after popular creators in your niche. Supplement your organic efforts with smart influencer collabs and paid advertising, deploying TikTok's robust interest, behavior, and location targeting capabilities. Most importantly, frequently analyze performance data to double down on what's working and tweak what's not through repeated testing.

While it may sound complex, user-friendly AI tools like invideo.io can streamline and simplify the entire process. Leverage automated video production, ad creative generation, intelligent audience-building, and real-time analytics monitoring. This AI-powered approach keeps your TikTok strategy data-driven and adaptable.

Stay focused on delighting your potential customers with entertaining, relevant videos optimized for engagement and conversions. With the right AI-powered tools and mindset, you can efficiently create scroll-stopping TikTok content that drives quantifiable ecommerce success. It's that simple.

The possibilities for growing your ecommerce business on TikTok are wide open. Don't get bogged down debating whether to handle the TikTok efforts in-house, hire a specialized agency, or outsource to freelance creators. Make that assessment swiftly based on your team's bandwidth and expertise.

You can launch a TikTok presence and start testing videos right away. Pay close attention to what content drives engagement and sales, then double down on those concepts. Continuously iterate based on real data until you find sustainable growth channels.

TikTok offers a prime opportunity to connect with a massive, engaged audience in their preferred digital space. You can cultivate an authentic community with an agile, data-driven mindset while profitably promoting your brand. By seizing TikTok's momentum now, your brand can get ahead of the curve and own this vital marketing channel.

Resources from this chapter:

1. Brandwatch: https://www.brandwatch.com/

2. Google Trends: https://trends.google.com/

3. Talkwalker: https://www.talkwalker.com/

4. TikTok Analytics: https://www.tiktok.com/analytics/

5. TikTok Ads Manager: https://ads.tiktok.com/

6. TikTok Creator Tools:
https://www.tiktok.com/creators/creator-portal/analytics

7. TikTok Pixel: https://ads.tiktok.com/help/article/pixel-events

Chapter 14

Personalization and Recommendation Engines

Personalization and recommendation engines have become indispensable tools for ecommerce businesses looking to deliver tailored experiences that resonate with individual customers. By harnessing the power of AI, these systems can analyze vast amounts of data, including browsing histories, purchase patterns, and preferences, to provide highly personalized product recommendations, targeted promotions, and customized content. While personalization is not a marketing channel itself, it is a powerful optimization tool that can significantly increase sales when implemented effectively across channels.

Imagine an ecommerce customer visiting your skincare products website, for example. With an AI-powered personalization engine like Clerk.io or Nosto integrated, as soon as they land on your site, the recommendations begin adapting in real time based on their behavior. The home page features a personalized banner showcasing the latest anti-aging serum you just launched, knowing this customer has previously viewed products in that category. As they browse moisturizers, the recommendations sidebar dynamically updates to suggest complementary serums, oils, and masks ideal for their specific skin type and concerns identified from past purchases.

This level of personalized curation enhances the shopping experience and directly drives sales. Research shows that personalized home page promotion can lift purchase rates by over 10%. Product recommendation engines have been proven to increase average order values by over 15% by suggesting complementary and frequently bought-together items.

Now, envision this shopper adding a cleanser to their cart. At checkout, personalized cross-sell prompts could recommend a brush set or specialized cleansing tool to pair with their selected product. After purchase, your personalized email flows take over, thanking them for their order while suggesting a full anti-aging regimen based on their latest buy. This creates a seamless, individualized journey that fosters customer loyalty and repeat purchases.

Personalization is just as powerful for ecommerce businesses in other verticals like home furnishings. With AI recommendation platforms like Vue.ai or Algolia, your customers could be presented with complete style recommendations for an entire room based on a single product they viewed, like a new sofa. Predictive algorithms analyze their tastes to suggest rugs, accent chairs, lamps, and art pieces that perfectly complement their initial pick both aesthetically and budgetarily.

Or imagine a shopper browsing trendy geometric-patterned rugs. With visual AI search tools like Syte or Visenze, your site could instantly display complementary products featuring similar motifs across home decor categories such as curtains, pillows, and even wallpaper. This intuitive experience allows customers to discover items that effortlessly match their styles.

➡ **AI PRO TIP** Implementing world-class personalization requires integrating dedicated AI solutions, but many streamlined options exist today. Platforms like Coveo and Algolia provide comprehensive search, recommendations, and personalization in a single integrated offering. Their AI models can be layered onto your existing ecommerce platform with relative ease.

Once deployed, it's critical to continuously optimize your AI's personalization capabilities. Regularly analyze performance data like click-through rates and conversion metrics for different recommendation types. Use this insight to strategically fine-tune your algorithms and business rules to steadily enhance relevance. Leverage AI and machine learning capabilities, allowing the models to self-tune recommendations based on observed patterns in customer behavior data.

Additionally, maintain human-in-the-loop controls, enabling your teams to manually make overrides and prioritize merchandising of specific product sets when needed. A balanced approach harnessing both AI automation and human expertise is crucial.

With the right personalization engine strategy, tangible ROI is almost immediate. Ecommerce leaders report seeing up to 30% revenue lift within the first few months. However, the long-term customer satisfaction gains are even more impactful.

Providing customers with a bespoke, intuitive shopping experience creates powerful brand affinity. The data shows that when interactions are personalized, customers significantly increase basket sizes, purchase frequencies, and lifetime values. One-size-fits-all browsing quickly becomes abhorred as customers become accustomed to your AI assistant beautifully understanding and catering to their individual tastes and needs.

In this chapter, I've recommended several powerful AI tools for implementing personalization and recommendation engines, such as Clerk.io, Nosto, Vue.ai, Algolia, Syte, Visenze, Coveo, and more. While each offers unique capabilities, you don't need to adopt them all at once. Depending on your business's specific needs and resources, you may want to start by exploring one solution that resonates most with you. Perhaps Clerk.io's all-in-one personalization suite aligns well with your ecommerce use case. If visual search and discovery are priorities, Syte and Visenze could be ideal first steps. The key is initiating your personalization journey with a proven AI partner and then expanding and refining your strategies over time based on performance data and customer feedback. Even beginning with a single personalization tool can unlock transformative potential.

In today's hyper-competitive ecommerce landscape, businesses embracing AI-driven personalization and recommendation engines have a powerful advantage in attracting, converting, and retaining satisfied, loyal customers. With many proven platforms available, the barriers to implementing these transformative capabilities have never been lower. Those who fail to leverage AI's personalization risk being outpaced and outmaneuvered by competitors who recognize its make-or-break importance.

Resources from this chapter:

1. Algolia: https://www.algolia.com/

2. Clerk.io: https://www.clerk.io/

3. Coveo: https://www.coveo.com/

4. Nosto: https://www.nosto.com/

5. Syte: https://www.syte.ai/

6. Visenze: https://visenze.com/

7. Vue.ai: https://vue.ai/

Chapter 15

Chatbots

Chatbots and conversational AI are revolutionizing the ecommerce landscape, providing businesses with powerful tools to deliver exceptional customer service and support while directly driving sales and growth. These AI-powered assistants are available 24/7, offering personalized experiences that cater to individual customer needs and preferences. As an ecommerce business owner, implementing chatbots and conversational AI solutions can streamline customer interactions, improve response times, and enhance overall customer satisfaction, ultimately leading to increased loyalty and revenue. While chatbots are not necessarily a marketing channel themselves, their ability to upsell products, recover abandoned carts, and facilitate purchases is why this chapter explores leveraging them as sales growth engines.

Envision a customer visiting your online store, intrigued by a particular product but seeking additional information or guidance. With a chatbot seamlessly integrated into your website, powered by leading natural language processing platforms like Salesforce Einstein, IBM Watson Assistant, or Amazon Lex, they can simply type their query, and the AI-powered assistant can provide detailed information, product recommendations, or even guide them through the purchase process step-by-step. This conversational and intuitive experience enhances the customer journey and reduces the workload on your support team, freeing them up to focus on more complex inquiries and tasks.

A key advantage of chatbots is driving additional purchases through personalized recommendations, upsells, cross-sells, and timely incentives. While platforms don't inherently generate personalized recommendations, they integrate to dynamically access and voice the suggestions your dedicated personalization engine, like Clerk.io or Nosto, has already computed for each customer.

For example, if a customer abandons their shopping cart without purchasing, your chatbot could automatically re-engage them with a reminder about the products they left behind. It could even incentivize them to complete the order by offering a limited-time discount or free shipping. For customers who do make a purchase, chatbots can analyze their order details and data to recommend complementary accessories and product bundles as high-value cross-sell opportunities.

Chatbots also enable creative ways to introduce new product lines and services. You could program them to offer customers exclusive product samples or free trial subscriptions - making personalized overtures at critical moments when shoppers are highly engaged. Chatbots ensure that existing loyalty program members stay actively engaged by providing notifications about exclusive rewards, point redemption options, and other VIP perks.

Here's how the personalization integration works: Your ecommerce site has a personalization engine like Clerk.io, which analyzes customer data to generate tailored product recommendations. When a customer initiates a chat conversation, the chatbot makes an API call to retrieve that visitor's unique recommendation data. It can then programmatically inject those personalized product suggestions at optimal moments.

For instance, if someone is purchasing a camera, the chatbot could say, "Based on the camera you're buying, here are some personalized lens and accessory recommendations that pair well and customers also love." It would display the specific products your personalization engine deems the best fits for that particular shopper's data and behavior. This integrated approach allows chatbots to have intelligent, hyper-personalized cross-sell conversations while avoiding having to rebuild sophisticated recommendation logic from scratch.

The personalized product recommendations can be updated in real time, too. If that same camera buyer continues shopping your site, the suggestions will adjust based on their evolving behavior and cart contents. The chatbot would resurface the latest personalized product bundle whenever they re-engage.

Leading brands like Sephora have already seen transformative results implementing AI chatbots to foster personalized shopping experiences that drive loyalty and sales. Sephora's bot provides virtual try-ons, shade matching, personalized skincare routines, and bundles - introducing customers to additional products and categories. In fashion ecommerce, chatbots enable virtual styling sessions with personalized size recommendations and outfit advice to reduce returns and cart abandonments.

As you explore solutions, many chatbot platforms offer advanced multilingual capabilities and direct integrations with messaging channels like Facebook, WhatsApp, and SMS. The integrations empower omnichannel brand engagements. Implementing chatbots also unlocks opportunities for sales teams by capturing prospect information and following up with personalized recommendations to nurture leads through your conversion funnels.

However, it's crucial to strike a balance between automation and the human touch. While chatbots excel at routine inquiries, you should provide escalation paths for customers to seamlessly transition complex issues to a live agent when needed. Continuously analyze chat transcripts and feedback to refine the chatbot's responses, ensuring cohesive conversational flows that accurately reflect your product information and brand voice.

By embracing chatbots' personalization and conversational commerce capabilities, you can transform customer service from a cost center into a powerful revenue generator. With the right strategy and integrated technology stack, AI assistants can provide exceptional experiences that keep customers engaged, driving bigger basket sizes, lower abandonment rates, and maximizing lifetime revenue across your entire brand ecosystem.

Resources from this chapter:

1. Amazon Lex: https://aws.amazon.com/lex/

2. Clerk.io: https://www.clerk.io/

3. IBM Watson Assistant: https://www.ibm.com/cloud/watson-assistant

4. Nosto: https://www.nosto.com/

5. Salesforce Einstein:
https://www.salesforce.com/products/einstein/overview/

Conclusion

There has never been a better time in history to be an entrepreneur, business owner, or marketer. Every week, technological advancements shock the news cycle with examples of how new small and large companies are creating amazing breakthroughs, often powered by AI.

We are witnessing amazing feats from tech companies like Neuralink, which implanted a chip in a man's brain, allowing him to control a computer with his mind like a Jedi using The Force. On a smaller scale, AI-powered tools can build websites in minutes, tasks for which people previously paid tens of thousands of dollars and took several months to accomplish.

A great example that embodies many of the principles from this book is Chamath Palihapitiya's incubator, 8090, which duplicates 80% of the features of enterprise software applications at a 90% reduction in cost by using AI tools and outsourcing.

Throughout this book, you have learned methods, tools, and strategies to leverage AI and marketing systems to implement strategies at lightning speed. Every week, the big LLM models like Claude, ChatGPT, Gemini, and others get better and better, supporting your efforts. You can ask these LLMs anything about ecommerce marketing or programming to help you implement tasks on the fly.

Simultaneously, developers are building new tools you can leverage at lightning speed, enabling you to use a combination of general AI capabilities with LLMs and more specific, narrow AI tools to help explode business areas like SEO and paid ads.

While these tools provide mind-blowing productivity and opportunities for you to dominate your ecommerce marketing space, new tools are on the horizon. So far, most AI tools have been copilots or support tools to help you work faster, better, and more efficiently. Conductor-style tools are about to emerge, where you will be able to instruct a manager or conductor-level tool to oversee a channel and make decisions that move your business forward. Imagine telling a conductor AI tool your SEO philosophies and instructing it to analyze your website and implement strategies on your behalf. The SEO conductor can optimize your website, build and post content, seek out and acquire backlinks, and do all the SEO work you would manually need to orchestrate in the past. Imagine letting an AI tool manage one of your marketing channels while you oversee its work as a backseat copilot. As scary as this may sound to some, a whole new level of productivity will emerge.

> Imagine telling an AI tool to read this book and implement all the strategies after creating a business plan for you to approve on executing each strategy.

It's exhilarating to be in this new AI-powered world. Ecommerce is the perfect playground to enjoy the benefits of being on the cutting edge of emerging tools and technologies.

All you have to do is work within the simple principles of this book. Find marketing channels to test, develop, and execute on those channels with lightning speed. Keep putting in the hard work until you find something profitable, then hire an agency to manage that channel or hire a freelancer or an in-house employee so you can continue to grow a variety of profitable marketing channels. Each channel will then compound by leveraging the success of the others. SEO and ads will drive people to your email list, which will help you continuously convert customers. Compound growth is hard to imagine for those who have yet to experience it, and it is especially powerful when multiple channels are feeding one main goal of growth, more customers, and more sales in a laser-focused, profitable, multichannel way.

When you develop a profitable channel and systems around it so that other people can manage it for you, you're creating a business that can be sold someday.

When you develop a profitable channel and systems around it so that other people can manage it for you, you're creating a business that can be sold someday.

The great thing is that in today's landscape, you don't need any prior skills to dominate in ecommerce marketing. All you need is a willingness to test, build channels, fail, learn, and keep going.

By the time you read this book, all the tools referenced might still be incredibly helpful or completely obsolete. It doesn't matter. You now have your path. Go crush it!

Keeping the Game Alive

Now you have everything you need to achieve explosive growth and success in ecommerce marketing, it's time to pass on your new found knowledge and show other readers where they can find the same help.

Simply by leaving your honest opinion of this book on Amazon, you'll show other ecommerce entrepreneurs and marketers where they can find the information they're looking for, and pass their passion for mastering digital marketing forward.

Thank you for your help. The game of ecommerce marketing is kept alive when we pass on our knowledge – and you're helping me to do just that.

Just visit the link below or scan the QR code to leave your review:

https://www.amazon.com/review/review-your-purchases/?asin=B0D6QMH58T

References

Adobe Analytics. (n.d.). Retrieved from
   https://www.adobe.com/analytics/analytics-cloud.html
Adacado. (n.d.). Retrieved from https://adacado.com/
Adroll. (n.d.). Retrieved from https://www.adroll.com/
Affistash. (n.d.). Retrieved from https://affistash.com/
Algolia. (n.d.). Retrieved from https://www.algolia.com/
Amazon Lex. (n.d.). Retrieved from https://aws.amazon.com/lex/
AspireIQ. (n.d.). Retrieved from https://www.aspireiq.com/
Awario. (n.d.). Retrieved from https://awario.com/
Bazaarvoice. (n.d.). Retrieved from https://www.bazaarvoice.com/
Bitly. (n.d.). Retrieved from https://bitly.com/
Brandwatch. (n.d.). Retrieved from https://www.brandwatch.com/
Buzz Sumo. (n.d.). Retrieved from https://buzzsumo.com/
Byword. (n.d.). Retrieved from https://byword.ai/
Cision. (n.d.). Retrieved from https://www.cision.com/
Claude. (n.d.). [AI software]. Retrieved from https://www.anthropic.com
Clerk.io. (n.d.). Retrieved from https://www.clerk.io/
Coveo. (n.d.). Retrieved from https://www.coveo.com/
Descript. (n.d.). [Web-based software]. Retrieved from
   https://www.descript.com/
Dibz.me. (n.d.). Retrieved from https://dibz.me/
emplifi.io. (n.d.). Retrieved from https://emplifi.io/
Fliki. (n.d.). Retrieved from https://fliki.ai/
Freelancer.com. (n.d.). Retrieved from https://www.freelancer.com/
Gemini. (n.d.). [AI software]. Retrieved from https://gemini.google.com/
Google. (n.d.). Submit a sitemap. Retrieved from
   https://www.google.com/search/docs/guides/submit-sitemap
Google AdWords. (n.d.). Retrieved from https://ads.google.com/
Google Analytics. (n.d.). Retrieved from https://analytics.google.com/
Google Ads Academy. (n.d.). Retrieved from
   https://ads.google.com/home/resources/

Google Campaign URL Builder. (n.d.). Retrieved from https://ga-dev-tools.appspot.com/campaign-url-builder/

Google Trends. (n.d.). Retrieved from https://trends.google.com/

Gravity Forms. (n.d.). Retrieved from https://www.gravityforms.com/

GumGum. (n.d.). Retrieved from https://gumgum.com/

Heepsy. (n.d.). Retrieved from https://www.heepsy.com/

Hootsuite. (n.d.). Retrieved from https://www.hootsuite.com/

Hoppy Copy. (n.d.). Retrieved from https://www.hoppycopy.co/

IBM Watson Assistant. (n.d.). Retrieved from https://www.ibm.com/cloud/watson-assistant

Impact. (n.d.). Retrieved from https://impact.com/

Intelligent Relations. (n.d.). Retrieved from https://www.intelligentrelations.com/

Invideo.io. (n.d.). Retrieved from https://invideo.io/

Justuno. (n.d.). Retrieved from https://www.justuno.com/

JustReachOut. (n.d.). Retrieved from https://justreachout.io/

Klaviyo. (n.d.). Retrieved from https://www.klaviyo.com/

Klear. (n.d.). Retrieved from https://www.meltwater.com/en

Link Whisper. (n.d.). Retrieved from https://linkwhisper.com/

LinkHunter.io. (n.d.). Retrieved from https://linkhunter.io/

Mango SEO.io. (n.d.). Retrieved from https://mangoseo.io/

Meadows, D. H. (2008). Thinking in systems: A primer. Chelsea Green Publishing

MediaMath. (n.d.). Retrieved from https://www.mediamath.com/

Mixpanel. (n.d.). Retrieved from https://mixpanel.com/

Monkey Learn's Review Analysis [Computer software]. (n.d.). Retrieved from https://monkeylearn.com/

Monitor Backlinks. (n.d.). Retrieved from https://monitorbacklinks.com/

MuckRack. (n.d.). Retrieved from https://muckrack.com/

NeoReach. (n.d.). Retrieved from https://neoreach.com/

Neulink. (n.d.). Retrieved from https://neuralinkdev.com/

Nosto. (n.d.). Retrieved from https://www.nosto.com/

Ocoyo. (n.d.). Retrieved from https://ocoyo.com/

OpenAI. (n.d.). ChatGPT [Computer software]. Retrieved from https://www.openai.com/chatgpt

Originality.ai. (n.d.). Retrieved from https://originality.ai/

PowerReviews. (2023). Survey: The ever-growing power of reviews (2023 edition). https://www.powerreviews.com/power-of-reviews-2023/#:~:text=Nine%20in%2010%20consumers%20say,not%20they%20purchase%20a%20product

Publisher Discovery. (n.d.). Retrieved from https://www.publisherdiscovery.com/

RADAAR. (n.d.). Retrieved from https://www.radaar.io/

Reddit. (n.d.). Retrieved from https://www.reddit.com/

Repurpose.io. (n.d.). Retrieved from https://repurpose.io/

Rockerbox. (n.d.). Retrieved from https://rockerbox.com/

Runway. (n.d.). Retrieved from https://runwayml.com/

Salesforce Einstein. (n.d.). Retrieved from https://www.salesforce.com/products/einstein/overview/

SEMrush. (n.d.). Retrieved from https://www.semrush.com/

ShareASale. (n.d.). Retrieved from https://www.shareasale.com/

Sivers, D. (2011). Anything you want. Penguin.

Sivers, D. (2020). How to live: 27 conflicting answers and one weird conclusion. WriteLife Publishing.

StealthGPT.ai. (n.d.). Retrieved from https://www.stealthgpt.ai/

Supertools.TheRundown.ai. (n.d.). Retrieved from https://supertools.therundown.ai/

Syte. (n.d.). Retrieved from https://www.syte.ai/

Talkwalker. (n.d.). Retrieved from https://www.talkwalker.com/

TINT. (n.d.). Retrieved from https://www.tintup.com/

TikTok Ads Manager. (n.d.). Retrieved from https://ads.tiktok.com/

TikTok Analytics. (n.d.). Retrieved from https://www.tiktok.com/analytics/

TikTok Creator Tools. (n.d.). Retrieved from https://www.tiktok.com/creators/creator-portal/analytics

TikTok Pixel. (n.d.). Retrieved from https://ads.tiktok.com/help/article/pixel-events

Tomoson. (n.d.). Retrieved from https://www.tomoson.com/

Traackr. (n.d.). Retrieved from https://www.traackr.com/

TribeTats.com. (n.d.). Retrieved from https://www.tribetats.com/

Trustpilot. (n.d.). Retrieved from https://www.trustpilot.com/

TubeBuddy. (n.d.). [Web-based software]. Retrieved from https://www.tubebuddy.com/

tweethunter.io. (n.d.). Retrieved from https://tweethunter.io/

Upfluence. (n.d.). Retrieved from https://upfluence.com/

VidIQ. (n.d.). [Web-based software]. Retrieved from https://vidiq.com/

Visenze. (n.d.). Retrieved from https://visenze.com/

Vue.ai. (n.d.). Retrieved from https://vue.ai/

Yotpo. (n.d.). Retrieved from https://www.yotpo.com/

Printed in Dunstable, United Kingdom